Fathers' Wit

Sometimes the greatest man you ever
meet … is the first one.

Fathers' Wit

FUNNY QUOTES ABOUT DADS

ROSEMARIE JARSKI

SevenOaks

This edition published in 2010

First published in Great Britain in 2005 by Prion
an imprint of the
Carlton Publishing Group
20 Mortimer Street
London W1T 3JW

Collection copyright © 2005 Rosemarie Jarski

The right of Rosemarie Jarski to be identified as the author of this
work has been asserted by her in accordance with the Copyright,
Designs and Patents Act 1998

A catalogue record for this book is available from the British Library

ISBN 978 1 85375 761 7

Typeset by e-type, Liverpool

Printed in the UK by CPI Mackays, Chatham, ME5 8TD

To the Best Dad in the World

Contents

Introduction

What has been proven to reduce crime, child poverty, mental illness, substance abuse, teenage pregnancy *and* requires no new taxes? The answer is Fatherhood. This being so, why is it that, with the exception of one-parent families and the elderly, there is no more beleaguered class in society today than fathers? Fathers are second-class citizens, sidelined, marginalized, ridiculed, castigated and undervalued. Listen to the news, pick up any newspaper, and you'd think there were only three kinds of dads: deadbeat, child abusers and deranged lunatics who dress up as superheroes and scale high buildings.

The Cult of Motherhood continues to flourish, but where are the worshippers at the Shrine of Fatherhood? Where is the biker with 'DAD' tattooed on his bicep? Where is the banner emblazoned with the slogan, 'Hello Dad'? When it comes to raising children, even the language is predicated against dads. 'Mothering' is defined as 'creating, nurturing and protecting'; 'Fathering' is defined as 'to procreate'. No emotional bond is implied. Fathers have the Mother of all Battles getting the recognition they deserve. The only time affection and gratitude are sanctioned is on Father's Day. Did you know that there are more reverse-charge calls on Father's Day than on any other day of the year? So, it has come to this: children are now charging their dad to tell him they love him.

No man can give birth to a child, but no woman can give a father's love. This treasury of fathers' wit is a Valentine to Dad, a celebration of the unique and vital role he plays in shaping our

9

Fathers' Wit

lives. Papa is a man of many parts – protector, provider, playmate and, in the case of most daughters, pushover. Every stage of fatherhood is explored, from family planning to empty nest, tackling the issues that *really* preoccupy fathers – such as sex, nappy-changing, sex, the family car, sex, how to stop your teenage daughters having sex and sex. Daughters, sons, wives and other family members offer sharp observations but, quite properly, most of the voices belong to fathers themselves. Old or new, good or bad, present or absent, Dad is here in his infinite variety. The only criterion for inclusion is that he should have some gem of wit to impart.

Fatherhood is a heavy responsibility so it can use a little light relief. The birth of a baby may be the happiest day of a man's life but it can also be the most terrifying. In an instant, everything changes. As Spock said (Mr not Dr), 'It's life, Jim, but not as we know it.' Sharing the funny side of the paternal predicament with some of those who've been there, done that, got the sick-stained T-shirt, can help allay fears and make the challenge seem less daunting. As Spock said (Dr not Mr), 'Laughter is preferable to tears since there is less cleaning up to do afterwards.' (Or was that Mrs?)

Some of the best and funniest insights come from TV dads. Fathers have a long pedigree on the small screen. *The Flintstones* featured one of the first pregnancies on prime-time US television. A 2002 survey showed that in 87 per cent of US sitcoms a father is the central character. Some of the most memorable TV pops include: Ben Cartwright (*Bonanza*); Albert Steptoe (*Steptoe and Son*); Fred Flintstone (*The Flintstones*); Homer Simpson (*The Simpsons*); Jim Royle (*The Royle Family*); Dan Conner (*Roseanne*); Cliff Huxtable (*The Cosby Show*); Gomez Addams (*The Addams Family*); Ozzy Osbourne (*The Osbournes*); Herman Munster (*The Munsters*); Alf Garnett (*Till Death Us Do Part*); Frank Spencer (*Some*

Mothers Do 'Ave 'Em); Ray Barone (*Everybody Loves Raymond*) ... how long do you have?

Watching these TV dads as we're growing up, having them right there in our living rooms, can exert a powerful if not unsettling influence. 'One year, *Bewitched* changed Darrins just like that,' recalls Rosie O'Donnell. 'For months I kept going up to my father saying, *Daddy*? Just checking.' Some children spend so long in front of the telly, it's possible they see more of the TV dads than of their own fathers. No bad thing in some cases. Who better to act *in loco parentis* than the warm, witty and wise Bill Cosby (provided they don't also copy his dubious taste in jumpers). TV dads offer valuable parenting tips – even if it's how *not* to do it. Yet, however bumbling or incompetent, most have their heart in the right place: the hapless Frank Spencer dotes on Little Jessica; 'Prince of Darkness' Ozzy Osbourne is practically Mr Mom to Kelly and Jack; and for all his many flaws, Homer Simpson loves Bart, Lisa and Maggie as much as beer, donuts and TV. Almost.

President George Bush *Père* famously declared that families would do better to follow the example of the Waltons than the Simpsons. Which father would you prefer? John Walton is the perfect paterfamilias, promoting virtues of thrift and self-improvement, dispensing homespun wisdom and never failing to say goodnight to his children. Homer Simpson is an overweight, workshy slob who forgets to pick up his son, Bart, from soccer practice and gets mad when someone spanks him as his own preferred form of corporal punishment is strangulation; he refuses to take his daughter to a bookfair ('If it doesn't have Siamese twins in a jar, it's not a fair'), and when asked if he likes his kids, says, 'What do you mean, *all* the time? Even when they're *nuts*?'

The American public gave their answer by voting Homer Simpson 'Best TV Dad' in an online poll. John Walton could only scrape ninth place. How could a jaundice-yellow cartoon character with no chin and a prominent overbite ever be considered a better father than Walton Mountain's paragon of paternity? Simple. Homer is more human. We can identify with him because he is *not* the perfect father, but he does try to do the best for his kids and they know that. Comedy plays a crucial part. Family life is particularly susceptible to sentimentalization. The humour of *The Simpsons* keeps it real and inoculates it against the schmaltz that infects *The Waltons*. *The Waltons* is 'feel-good' but vapid and hollow at heart. *The Simpsons* is genuinely heart-warming and uplifting. George Bush and his like may denounce it as subversive and setting a bad example, but there are few shows with a deeper moral core. The Simpsons family is neither rich nor perfect but they *are* happy. And that's what is *really* subversive, what really riles our betters – the idea that you don't have to be rich or perfect to be happy.

The Simpsons offers a rounded view of average family life, showing that, while it can be wonderful, caring and fun, it can also be horrible, selfish and cruel. What lies at its heart, though, is love. 'Love,' said Peter Ustinov, 'is an act of endless forgiveness, a tender look which becomes a habit.' In families, forgiveness is in daily demand, and particularly so in father–son relationships. The parable of the Prodigal Son never goes out of fashion. Ernest Hemingway wrote a poignant short story called 'The Capital of the World' about a Spanish father who becomes estranged from his son. After an argument, the son leaves home and goes to Madrid. Years later, the father is desperate for a reconciliation and travels to Madrid. But he is unable to trace his son. More in hope than expectation, he places an ad in the local newspaper: 'Dear Paco. All is forgiven. Meet me Tuesday at noon in front of the Hotel Montana. Papa.' The father arrives in the square at the appointed time, and finds 800 young men named Paco all hoping to be reunited with their fathers.

'Romance fails us and so do friendships, but the relationship of Father and Child, less noisy than all the others, remains indelible and indestructible, the strongest relationship on earth,' wrote Theodor Reik. The quotes in this collection bear witness to that unbreakable bond.

One thing to emerge in the course of compiling this collection is something that might be called Dad Humour. Common to all fathers, crossing centuries, continents and cultures, it's a curious blend of cynicism, silliness and more corn than Kansas in August. All kids start by thinking *their* dad is the funniest person on earth. Then they grow up and realize that Dad Humour, like Dad Dancing, is the most toe-curlingly embarrassing torture a father can ever inflict on his poor innocent offspring. The irony is that children who spend their teenage years turning beetroot-red at dad's lame gags later find themselves helplessly repeating the very same lame gags to their own children. *Plus ça change* …

Unlike many books about fathers, this one doesn't set out to be instructive or prescriptive; just funny. But since humour is truth-telling, it ends up telling you a lot more than many of those bossy childcare manuals. A great deal of wisdom is wrapped up in these nuggets of fatherly wit.

So what's the secret of being a good dad – apart from the obvious but critical, 'Know when to stop tickling'? The simple answer seeps through these pages by osmosis … Be There. To be in your child's memories tomorrow you have to be in their lives today. Not just for the so-called milestones like birthdays, concerts and graduations, but for those seemingly small everyday moments such as pushing a swing, sharing a pizza, reading a bedtime story. After all, you never know when you're making a memory. Boswell, the biographer of Samuel Johnson, would often refer to a day in his youth when his father took him fishing. He remembered the trip as a special time when his father taught him many lessons he carried with him through life. And how did Boswell's father remember the same excursion? The entry in his journal for that day records just a single sentence: 'Gone fishing today with my son; a day wasted.'

What is a Father?

Directly after God in heaven comes Papa.

Wolfgang Amadeus Mozart

A father is first a curiosity, then an amusement-park ride, then a referee, and finally, a bank.

Esquire *magazine*

A father is a cash-point machine in trousers.

Martin Hart

A father is a man who carries photographs where his money used to be.

Anon

A father is a banker provided by nature.

French proverb

A father is a giant shock absorber, there to protect the family from the ruts and bumps on the road of life.

W. Bruce Cameron

Daddies are for catching spiders.

Molly, aged 4

A dad is the one that gets your Maths homework wrong.

Jane, aged 8

Father is the guy who's quick to appear with the camera and just as quick to disappear when there's a diaper to be changed.

Joan Rivers

Fathers' Wit

A father is a man who prefers sleep over sex.

Ralph Anderson

A dad is someone you can find in the pub.

Louis, aged 7

Father is the thoughtful man who will suggest putting vodka in a baby's bottle when he's crying.

Joan Rivers

A dad is the one who, after a roast dinner on Sunday, falls asleep in his comfy armchair with the newspaper over his face, while mum does the washing up.

Jamie, aged 10

A father is something mythical and infinitely important: a protector, who keeps a lid on all the chaotic and catastrophic possibilities of life.

Tom Wolfe

When I was a little kid, a father was like the light in the refrigerator: every house had one, but no one really knew what either of them did once the door was shut.

Erma Bombeck

A father should be a man of many faces – an artist, a philosopher, a statesman and, above all, a prolific dispenser of good sense and justice.

Adlai Stevenson

A dad is a man who says, 'I'll put up a conservatory!', 'I'll decorate the box-room!' 'I'll mow the lawn!' but never gets round to it because he prefers playing golf and going down the pub.

Chris Miller

What is a Father?

A father is a plaster that cures all the ills of his children.

Sean Cooper

A father is a giant from whose shoulders you can see for ever.

Perry Garfinkel

Any man can be a father. It takes someone special to be a dad.

Anon

A good father is a little bit of a mother.

Lee Salk

Having children makes you no more a father than having a violin makes you a violinist.

Anon

A dad is someone who helps you with your times tables and knows all the capitals of all the countries in the entire world.

Scott Willis

A dad is someone you can act daft with and practise your judo moves on.

Jordan, aged 8

The thing to remember about fathers is, they're men. A girl has to keep it in mind: they are dragon-seekers, bent on improbable rescues. Scratch any father, you find someone chock-full of qualms and romantic terrors, believing change is a threat – like your first shoes with heels on, like your first bicycle it took such months to get.

Phyllis McGinley

A dad is someone who loves you more than anyone else except your mum.

Melissa, aged 9

Fatherhood

What's it called when you're damned if you do, and damned if you don't? Oh, yes, fatherhood.

Paul Hennessy, 8 Simple Rules for Dating My Teenage Daughter

I won't lie. Fatherhood isn't easy like motherhood. But I wouldn't trade it for anything. Except for some mag wheels.

Homer Simpson, The Simpsons

Fatherhood is pretending the present you love most is soap-on-a-rope.

Bill Cosby

My idea of fatherhood is sending a telegram from Abyssinia saying, 'Have you had your child yet, and what have you called it?'

Evelyn Waugh

The great thing about being a guy is that bathroom lines are shorter. You can open your own jars. Your butt is not a fact in a job interview. All your orgasms are real. Foreplay is optional. You can sit with your knees apart no matter what you're wearing. Not liking a person does not preclude having great sex with them. There's always a game on somewhere. But most of all, being a father.

Anon

A father's job is not to get tired of what he has a right to get tired of: for example, small people who keep doing things that you tell them not to do, and when you ask them why they keep doing these things, they reply, 'I don't know.'

Bill Cosby

Fatherhood

Being a father is like doing drugs – you smell bad, get no sleep and spend all your money on them.

Paul Bettany

Life doesn't come with an instruction book – that's why we have fathers.

H. Jackson Brown Sr

Men will now get up and walk with the baby in the middle of the night, change its diapers, and give it a bottle, but in their heart of hearts they still think they shouldn't have to.

Rita Rudner

I'm nostalgic for a time when dads never changed nappies, never read bedtime stories, couldn't speak to their children and were only expected to administer corporal punishment.

Ted Searle

There are to us no ties at all just in being a father. It's the practice of parenthood that makes you feel that, after all, there may be something in it.

Heywood Broun

After all, I'm your father. It's true if it hadn't been me it would have been someone else. But that's no excuse.

Samuel Beckett

I make it a rule to pat all children on the head as I pass by – in case it is one of mine.

Augustus John

I've got more paternity suits than leisure suits.

Engelbert Humperdinck

Yes, I did father a child with Wendy Craig. It all happened in the 1960s. We were very excitable then.

John Mortimer

My dream would be to build a 2,000-foot statue of Homer Simpson with a revolving head and a restaurant inside it. A monument to fatherhood.

Matt Groening, creator of The Simpsons

To Breed or Not to Breed?

FAMILY PLANNING

Kids, it's the biggest decision you'll ever make, isn't it? That and whether to be a lager or a bitter drinker.

Tony, Men Behaving Badly

You need a licence to buy a dog, to drive a car – hell, you need a licence to catch a fish. But they'll let any jackass be a father.

Martin Abbott

You wake up one day and say, 'You know what, I don't think I ever need to sleep or have sex again.' Congratulations, you're ready to have children.

Ray Romano

Parents are the very last people who ought to be allowed to have children.

Samuel Butler

– Oh, come on, Miranda. I want a baby. It'd be fun.
– It's not like owning a football table, Steve.

Steve Brady and Miranda Hobbes, Sex and the City

Having a child is surely the most beautifully irrational act that two people in love can commit.

Bill Cosby

To Breed or Not to Breed?

How could Tristan and Isolde, or Romeo and Juliet, have survived if there had been a child? All the poetry would have been lost in irritation at feeding time.

Peter Ustinov

It is one of the great urban myths that people get pregnant in order to have children.

Menzies Campbell

Why does a man want a child? Is it to perpetuate the species? Is the child a pet substitute? Is it to prove that he has had sex at least once?

Jeremy Hardy

If I do want children it's because I love Lucy. That's the only way I can think about it. If I try to think of kids in the abstract I very quickly come up against no sleep and vomit in my personal stereo.

Ben Elton, Inconceivable

I think we should have a baby. Other people do it. I'd have someone to do my shopping for me when I'm old.

Gary, Men Behaving Badly

My father had children because they were a by-product of sex.

Carrie Fisher

Rachel and Ross are so irresponsible. Their baby is the product of a bottle of Merlot and a five-year-old condom.

Monica Geller, Friends

I had a dream that all the victims of the Pill came back … Boy, were they mad.

Steven Wright

Fathers' Wit

Familiarity breeds contempt – and children.

Mark Twain

I have certainly seen more men destroyed by the desire to have a wife and child and to keep them in comfort than I have seen destroyed by drink or harlots.

William Butler Yeats

Men have children to prove they aren't impotent, or at least that some of their friends aren't.

P. J. O'Rourke

When my son, Jake, was born, one of my first thoughts was oh good, someone to go to football matches with.

Hunter Davies

Warren Beatty only had children so he can meet some babysitters.

David Letterman

Children are the only form of immortality that we can be sure of.

Peter Ustinov

The reason most people have kids is because they get pregnant.

Mark Ryan

Humans are the only animals that have children on purpose with the exception of guppies, who like to eat theirs.

P. J. O'Rourke

It seems to me that two people have a baby just to see what they can make, like a kind of erotic arts and crafts.

Bill Cosby

To Breed or Not to Breed?

What's a home without children? Quiet.

Henny Youngman

What have I got against having children? In the first place there isn't enough room. In the second place they seem to start by mucking up their parents' lives, and then go on in the third place to muck up their own. In the fourth place it doesn't seem right to bring them into a world like this. In the fifth place and in the sixth place I don't like them very much in the first place. OK?

Simon Gray, Otherwise Engaged

A son of my own! Oh, no, no, no! Let my flesh perish with me, and let me not transmit to anyone the boredom and the ignominiousness of life.

Gustave Flaubert

I don't like children, but I like to make them.

Groucho Marx

Parenting, there's a tough job. Easy job to get though. I think most people love the interview. You don't even have to dress for it.

Steve Bruner

I like children. Properly cooked.

W. C. Fields

As a child, I thought I hated everybody, but when I grew up I realized it was just children I didn't like.

Philip Larkin

Learning to dislike children at an early age saves a lot of expense and aggravation later in life.

Robert Byrne

Fathers' Wit

Of children, as of procreation – the pleasure momentary, the posture ridiculous, the expense damnable.

Evelyn Waugh

He that doth get a wench with child and marries her afterwards it is as if a man should shit in his hat and then clap it on his head.

Samuel Pepys

Then Trey told the lie that all parents-to-be have to tell themselves in order to procreate: '*Our* kids will be different to everybody else's.'

Carrie Bradshaw, Sex and the City

– Anthea, remind me what's so good about being a child-free single person?
– Well, you can keep everything neat and tidy and smart around the home. And people don't visit, so there's lots of time to sit and read my gardening magazines and nod off with Melody Radio on. And, of course, although I sometimes have a bit of a cry, that usually makes me feel better, and then I go mad and have sardines on toast to really cheer me up.

Anthea, Men Behaving Badly

I abominate the sight of children so much that I have always had the greatest regard for the character of Herod.

Lord Byron

When asked why he did not become a father, Thales answered, 'Because I am fond of children.'

Diogenes Laertius

If your parents never had children, chances are you won't either.

Clarence Day

To Breed or Not to Breed?

My parents waited ten years for me; that's the way they always put it, as if I were a late train to a place they desperately wanted to go.

Kitty Florey

My husband is English and I'm American. I wonder what our children would be like. They'd probably be rude, but disgusted by their own behaviour.

Rita Rudner

The only time I feel broody is when I see parents and children boarding the plane first or in the supermarket car park when I can't find a space.

John Mason

We're not sure about kids yet. They cost a lot of money, don't they? Maybe we can get one who's about 22 and a solicitor so he can bring a good wage in.

Ricky Gervais

– Norm, how come you and Vera never had any kids?
– I can't, Coach.
– Gee, I'm sorry, Norm.
– I look at Vera … and I just can't.

'Coach' Pantusso and Norm Peterson, Cheers

I suppose the big question is, do I really want to have children with a man who has a Fungus the Bogeyman pillowcase?

Dorothy, Men Behaving Badly

The problem with the gene pool is that there is no lifeguard.

Steven Wright

Men are like photocopiers. You need them for reproduction but that's about it.

Anon

Fathers' Wit

I'd like to start a family, but you have to have a date first.

Larry David

Why should I have a kid? I already have girlfriends who call me 'Daddy'.

Bill Maher

I never want to get married and have children because I wouldn't want another me.

Simon Cowell

Childlessness has many obvious advantages. One is that you need not spend $200,000 to send anyone to college. But the principal advantage of the nonparental life-style is that on Christmas Eve, you need not be struck dumb by the three most terrifying words that the government allows to be printed on any product: 'Some assembly required.'

John Leo

The only way my wife and I can afford to have kids is if she breast-fed them for 18 years.

Paul Alexander

– Pregnancy is one of the taboo subjects. We can spend two
  days arguing about the name of the fifth Osmond, but we
  can't talk about whether we should give life to another
  human being.
– Brian. Brian Osmond. Trust me.

Dorothy and Gary, Men Behaving Badly

My wife and I don't want kids. If we have a sudden urge to spank someone, we'll spank each other.

Danny Liebert

Literature is mostly about having sex and not much about having children. Life is the other way round.

David Lodge

To Breed or Not to Breed?

I really want to have a child because Christmas without one is rubbish.

Hugh Grant

The time not to become a father is 18 years before a world war.

E. B. White

Parenting may not be for you if you consider a Happy Meal to be any meal that includes a dry Martini.

Anon

A vasectomy means not ever having to say you're sorry.

Larry Adler

I decided to have a vasectomy after a family vote on the matter. The kids voted for it eleven to three.

Bob Fraser

Buy me and stop one.

Advert for condoms

My views on birth control are somewhat distorted by the fact that I was the seventh of nine children.

Robert F. Kennedy

Children are nature's very own form of birth control.

Dave Barry

Never have children, only grandchildren.

Gore Vidal

My husband and I have discovered a foolproof method of birth control. An hour with the kids before bedtime.

Roseanne Barr

Fathers' Wit

Oh, what a tangled web we weave when first we practise to conceive.

Don Herold

Don't you just hate those couples who go round telling everybody that they're 'trying' for a baby. We can do without the visual.

Pete Brown

- Do you know, a yoghurt pot full of my semen could repopulate the whole of Ireland?
- Haven't they had a tragic enough history without you turning up at the border with your yoghurt pot?

Gary and Dorothy, Men Behaving Badly

Every sperm is sacred,
Every sperm is great;
If a sperm is wasted,
God gets quite irate.

Father, Monty Python's The Meaning of Life

My wife says the best thing about me having a low sperm count is that she doesn't have to have sex with me to get pregnant.

Tom Arnold

My husband and I went to one of the fertility clinics where they charge you millions of dollars every time your husband jerks off into a jar. He was too uncomfortable there to perform, so to get a sample he went back to his old room in his parents' house.

Karen Haber

I have nothing against sperm banks, but they really should get rid of those automatic teller machines.

David Corrado

I don't agree with all this artificial insemination. I prefer the old-fashioned way of having children. By accident.

Rick Stone

I am married to Beatrice Salkeld, painter. We have no children, except me.

Brendan Behan

Great Expectations

PREGNANCY

– Jimmy, I've got a surprise for you.
– Oh, no! Last time you said that you'd just finished peeing on a stick.

Beth and Jimmy Cox, Rock Me Baby

– Woody, I'm pregnant.
– With a baby?

Woody and Susan Boyd, Cheers

– We're going to have a baby. That's my Christmas present to you.
– All I needed was a tie.

Woody Allen

My wife just told me the good news – I'm going to be a dad for the first time. The bad news – we already have two kids.

Brian Kiley

I assumed, prior to the experience, that I would be the most unlikely father. When Paula rang me and I was in New York she was blabbing, saying, 'Oh, I'm pregnant,' and I went 'Oh fuck!' but I didn't actually say that. I said,

Fathers' Wit

'That's fantastic!' I just stared at myself in the mirror and kept saying, 'What the fuck now? You're going to be a father.' But then I wondered would I do all right? I knew it was the long haul, and I thought, 'Why not? And what better babe to do it with? It's going to be a hoot!'

Bob Geldof

My husband only got it when I told him we'd be downloading some new software in nine months' time.

Laura Greene

I'd been cast in the part of my life … but I'd never heard of the leading man. I was definitely playing a supporting role. Still, I'd never had a better part, and only once one as good – in the sequel. I was to be a father!

Charlton Heston

It is much easier to become a father than to be one.

Kent Nerburn

I am a terrible realist about becoming a father. If it's a nice baby, obviously I will be over the moon, but I'm not going to be over the moon until I know what it's like.

Louis de Bernières

No smoking, no drinking, no pills – pregnancy is a pain. But only for the mother! We dads can get as legless, obese and high as we damn well please!

Richard Taylor

My wife is pregnant but she refuses to give up smoking. She says she's smoking for two now.

Mervin Allen

Why am I excited to become a father? Two words: Swedish nanny.

David Letterman

Great Expectations

I hope someday you know the indescribable joy of having children – and of paying someone else to raise them.

Gomez, Addams Family Values

It's not easy to juggle a pregnant wife and a troubled child, but somehow I manage to fit in eight hours of TV a day.

Homer Simpson

Pregnancy is amazing. To think that you can create a human being just with the things you have around the house.

Shang

I can't wait to have a kid. I'll introduce them to classical music like Hendrix and the Rolling Stones.

Roger Howe

What's fatter than a pot-bellied pig after a cruise? My wife in seven months.

David Letterman

I do wish my husband would stop calling me Madame Ovary.

Alice Kane

– Don't worry, I'll be there for you, with hot towels.
– That'll be handy if I give birth in a Chinese restaurant.

Gary and Dorothy, Men Behaving Badly

– Have you seen the sonogram … isn't it amazing?
– What are we supposed to be seeing here?
– I dunno, but I think it's about to attack the Enterprise.

Ross Geller, Joey Tribbiani and Chandler Bing, Friends

We tried to find traces of family resemblance in the sonogram. I said it looked just like her mother – if she were bald, had no eyelids and was floating in amniotic fluid. She said from the other side it looked just like my father. Presuming, of course, he was a Hawaiian prawn.

Paul Reiser

I found the fathering book in the bookstore under 'Psychological Disorders'.

David Letterman

I refuse to buy any fathering book that includes anything about childbirth.

David Letterman

You have to be mad to have children. The less you know about what it will really be like, the better, otherwise no one would ever do it.

Nigel Planer

All the time during the pregnancy when I was supposed to be reading baby books and taking baby classes didn't go totally to waste because I did use the time to shop for the perfect video camera.

Paul Reiser

I've spent 15 years raising the kids. The only thing I'd use the parenting manual for is to whack their butts.

Earl Sinclair, Dinosaur

So you don't still think test-tube babies have to smash their way out of their test tube to be born? Or that you have to have sex twice to have twins?

Dorothy to Gary, Men Behaving Badly

There was a time in my life when I would have *killed* for reliable information about the uterus. But having discussed it in detail at childbirth classes, and having seen actual full-colour pictures of it, it's lost a lot of its sparkle for me.

Dave Barry

I'm preparing for the baby. I'm busy putting childproof caps on all the bottles of booze.

David Letterman

It takes many nails to build a cradle, but only one screw to fill it.

Anon

Let me explain something to you. There is no such thing as a trimester. There's actually just one long 40-year-mester.

Al Bundy, Married … With Children

– Did you watch the tape of the woman giving birth?
– Oh boy, before this, the most disturbing thing I ever saw was my dad doing tequila shots off the pool boy. Now I'd gladly use that image as my screensaver.

Joey Tribbiani and Chandler Bing, Friends

– Do you feel the butterfly of life fluttering within you?
– It's either that or gas.

Frasier Crane and Lilith Sternin, Cheers

When she was pregnant, my wife's craving was not to be pregnant.

Jez Tyler

During her pregnancy, my wife only had one craving: my death.

Richard Taylor

Before you have kids, you'd better have prepared your answers for some tricky questions: Dad, did *you* inhale?

Roger Howe

Smear peanut butter on the sofa and curtains. Rub your hands in the wet flowerbed and then on the walls. Place a fish stick behind the couch and leave it there all summer. Congratulations, you are prepared for parenthood.

Anon

Preparing for fatherhood: go to the nearest chemist. Set your wallet on the counter. Ask the clerk to help himself. Now proceed to the nearest food store. Go to the head office and arrange for your paycheque to be directly deposited to the store. Purchase a newspaper. Go home and read it quietly for the last time.

Anon

Best thing I did when preparing to become a father was build myself a shed. It's the perfect place to escape to when it all gets too much.

Gareth Evans

Unto Us a Child is Born

BIRTH

He became a father today. There'll be hell to pay if his wife finds out.

Milton Berle

I remember so clearly us going into hospital so Victoria could have Brooklyn. I was eating a Lion bar at the time.

David Beckham

Just as I was about to give birth, Mick arrived at the hospital bearing diamond earrings and caviar. The wives and nurses were very excited to find him there with a pot of caviar, and asked for lemon slices and toast.

Jerry Hall, ex-Mrs Jagger

Unto Us a Child is Born

Should a father be present at the birth of his child? It's all any reasonable child can expect if Dad is present at the conception.

Joe Orton

I think the husband should always be in the delivery room. Along with the child's father.

Maureen Murphy

I'm told I'm a 'coach' and my job is to remind my wife to breathe. When was the last time you had to be reminded to breathe? It's like saying, 'Digest!'

Robert Klein

Men come into the delivery room and say, 'Breathe.' Is that really a sharing experience? If I ever have a baby I want my husband to be on the table next to me, at least getting his legs waxed.

Rita Rudner

I once heard two ladies going on and on about how painful childbirth is and how men don't know what real pain is. I asked if either of them ever got themselves caught in a zipper.

Emo Philips

I was fully prepared for being present at the birth of my first child: I watched the movie *Alien* a couple of times.

Bob Hayden

The old system of having a baby was much better than the new system, the old system being characterized by the fact that the man didn't have to watch.

Dave Barry

Men didn't attend the birth in my day. I think because the baby comes out of a lady's rude area.

George, Men Behaving Badly

Fathers' Wit

If men had to have babies, they would only ever have one each.

Princess Diana

If men knew their bellies might swell as if they were suffering from end-stage cirrhosis, that they would have to go nearly a year without a stiff drink, a cigarette or even an aspirin, then I'm sure that pregnancy would be classified as a sexually transmitted disease.

Barbara Ehrenreich

If men could get pregnant, abortion would be a sacrament.

Florynce Kennedy

Let's face it, if God had meant men to have children, he would have given them PVC aprons.

Victoria Wood

I fulfilled my duty in the delivery room: I stayed upright.

Frank Mungbeam

If you'd like more technical details on the childbirth process, I suggest you view one of those prairie dramas on TV wherein some wispy-haired pioneer woman goes into labour during a blizzard. Nothing brings on labour like a prairie blizzard.

Dave Barry

For a father, a home birth is preferable. That way you're not missing anything on television.

Jeremy Hardy

I told my wife I don't want to be there at the birth. I don't see why my evening should be ruined too.

Dennis Wolfberg

Unto Us a Child is Born

I said to my wife, 'Give me one good reason why I should be in the delivery room with you while you're in labour.' She said, 'Alimony.'

Paul Mather

When my wife was giving birth, she tried the breathing exercises and they were really effective for, oh, I'd say 15, even 20, seconds. Then she switched to the more traditional method, which is screaming for drugs.

Dave Barry

Your partner will swear like you have never heard her swear before, and then affront your masculinity by falling in love with the anaesthetist. Anaesthetists possess a means of seduction more potent than any aphrodisiac or native oyster. It is called an epidural.

Adam Lindsay

When Sarah pleaded for the epidural, I reminded her, 'Sweetheart, it's just like the pain I had when my tooth was pulled.' She said, 'Oh, yeah? Now imagine that tooth was in your ass!'

Cuba Gooding Jr

When the big natural childbirth moment came, I did what came naturally: I fainted.

Alan Thicke

My wife beckoned me closer and whispered, 'I want you close to me now, honey – so I can grab your testicles and you can get an idea of the pain I'm going through right now.'

Don Ware

You have this myth, as the father, that if you're there at the birth, you're sharing the birthing experience. Unless you're circumcising yourself with a chain saw, I don't think so. Unless you're opening an umbrella up your ass, I don't think so.

Robin Williams

Fathers' Wit

It is easier to bear a child once a year than to shave every day.

Russian proverb

My wife, God bless her, was in labour for 32 hours, and I was faithful to her the entire time.

Jonathan Katz

For men, childbirth is that cruellest of combinations: stressful and boring.

Marcus Berkmann, Fatherhood: The Truth

Watching a baby being born is a little like watching a wet St Bernard coming in through the cat flap.

Jeff Foxworthy

We had a caesarean section. That's when the baby pops out like toast.

Bobcat Goldthwait

Caesarean section? Isn't that the part of the Roman Colosseum where the emperors sat?

George Carlin

Blokes can watch but can't know what it feels like to have a baby. One woman I spoke to said a caesarean feels like someone doing the washing up in your stomach.

Tony Parsons

During the caesarean, when the doctor cauterized the veins and smoke started billowing from Heather's stomach, I got queasy. But I had confidence that this was all routine for the doctors when I heard them discussing the college football game.

Richie Sambora

I had a caesarean section and my husband, an Italian restaurateur, was present throughout. After it was over he

whispered to me, 'Linda, I must tell you … I saw your liver.
I know I did. I recognize it from the restaurant.'

Lynda Bellingham

The doctor said, 'Would you like to cut the cord?' I said,
'Isn't there someone more qualified?'

Bobcat Goldthwait

– We have a new baby, can you guess what it is?
– A boy.
– No, guess again.

Gracie Allen and George Burns

Everyone loved little Margaret. Dad said there must have
been a holiday in Heaven the day this baby was born.

Frank McCourt, Angela's Ashes

You had not been bathed when I held you. The obstetrician
gave you to me so she could examine your mother … I
held you against my breast. You smelt of love-making.

Peter Carey

I couldn't have been more besotted than if it had been the
Baby Jesus himself; in fact, I fully expected the christening
gifts to be gold, frankincense and myrrh.

Mitchell Hoyle

When I saw Sophia Rose, I really understood for the first
time what it's like to look into an infant's eyes and know
you would die for that person.

Sylvester Stallone

The first handshake in life is the greatest of all: the clasp of
an infant's fist around a parent's finger.

Mark Beltaire

Never will a time come when the most marvellous recent invention is as marvellous as a newborn baby.

Carl Sandburg

This moment of meeting seemed to be a birthtime for both of us: her first and my second life.

Laurie Lee

I remember the very first time I ever held my son in my arms as a newborn. Everything else in the universe melted away. There was just a father, a son, and the distant sound of my wife saying, 'If you ever come near me again, I'll drop you with a deer rifle.'

Frasier Crane, Frasier

It's like getting ready for your own birth. Nothing prepares you. When those eyes meet your eyes – I was feeling things I never had feelings like before. But let us make no mistake as to why the baby is here: it is here to replace *us*. We'll see who's wearing the diapers when all this is over.

Jerry Seinfeld

I think the strangest and strongest sensation of your life will be hearing for the first time the thin cry of your own child. For a moment you have the feeling of being double; but there is something more, quite impossible to analyse – perhaps the echo in a man's heart of all the sensations felt by all the fathers and mothers of his race at a similar instant in the past. It is very tender, but also a very ghostly feeling.

Lafcadio Hearn

I had to restrain myself from grabbing passers-by in the street and shaking them and shouting in their faces, '*I'm a father! Complete! Not firing blanks! My biological destiny fulfilled!*'

Jake Ferrari

You Must Have Been a Beautiful Baby

I married your mother because I wanted children. Imagine my disappointment when you came along.

Groucho Marx

Fortunately, my parents were intelligent, enlightened people. They accepted me for what I was, a punishment from God.

David Steinberg

I have never understood the fear of some parents about babies getting mixed up in a hospital. What difference does it make as long as you get a good one?

Heywood Broun

When I drove home from the hospital after my baby was born, for the first time in my life I obeyed all the traffic laws. I had another life to take care of.

Will Smith

I love to think that the day you're born, you're given the world as a birthday present.

Leo Buscaglia

You Must Have Been a Beautiful Baby

All babies are supposed to look like me – at both ends.

Winston Churchill

I was so ugly at birth that the midwife took one look at me, turned, and slapped my father.

Joan Rivers

Fathers' Wit

George and Melinda's new sprog is ugly as a monkey's arse. George calls it Prune which I think is fair, although 'old man's scrotum' would probably be closer to the mark.

Ben Elton, Inconceivable

I bet your father spent the first year of your life throwing rocks at the stork.

Groucho Marx

My new son has a face like that of an ageing railway porter who is beginning to realize that his untidiness has meant that he'll never get that ticket–collector's job he's been after for twenty years.

Kingsley Amis

I can see that it is a very homely baby indeed. Still I never see many babies that I consider rose geraniums for looks, anyway.

Damon Runyon

Introduced to his child, he recoiled with a startled 'Oi!' The only thing that prevented a father's love from faltering was the fact that there was in his possession a photograph of himself at the same early age, in which he, too, looked like a homicidal fried egg.

P. G. Wodehouse

My father thought I was so ugly he carried around the photograph of the kid who came with his wallet.

Rodney Dangerfield

All babies start off looking like the last tomato in the fridge.

Ben Elton, Inconceivable

You Must Have Been a Beautiful Baby

Thank goodness he hasn't got ears like his father!

Queen Elizabeth II, on first seeing Prince William

No baby is admired sufficiently to please the parents.

E. V. Lucas

I find that the most successful approach to the subject of babies is to discuss them as though they were hams; the firmness of the flesh, the pinkness of the flesh, the even distribution of fat, the sweetness and tenderness of the whole, and the placing of bone are the things to praise.

Samuel Marchbanks

I think God made babies cute so we don't eat them.

Robin Williams

What's tough about seeing people when they have a new baby is that you have to try and match their level of enthusiasm. They're always so excited. Just once I would like to meet a couple who say, 'Frankly, you know, we're not that happy with him. We think we made a big mistake. We should've gotten an aquarium. You want him? We've had enough.'

Jerry Seinfeld

I don't know why it is, but I've never been able to bear with fortitude anything in the shape of a kid with golden curls. Confronted with one, I feel the urge to step on him or drop things from a height.

P. G. Wodehouse

I was an ugly kid. My dad never took me to the zoo. He said if they wanted me, they'd come get me.

Rodney Dangerfield

I have good-looking kids. Thank goodness my wife cheats on me.

Rodney Dangerfield

In the Name of the Father

CHOOSING A NAME

– What's your name?
– Alex.
– Alex what?
– ander.

Alexander and Alexander Clayton Jr

Men name their children after themselves; women don't. Have you ever met a Sally Junior?

Rita Rudner

Naming our baby was a trial. I seize up when I have to name a document on my computer.

Jeff Stilson

Chandler *Muriel* Bing … your parents never gave you a chance, did they?

Joey Tribbiani, Friends

– What about Desmond?
– 'Desmond Crane, you are hereby sentenced to …' No, I don't like it.

Niles and Daphne Crane, Frasier

In the Name of the Father

– Okay, how about Ruth?
– I'm sorry, are we having an 89-year-old woman?

Rachel Green and Ross Geller, Friends

Gary still likes Cindy-Sue for a girl and Scamp for a boy. So I may have to kill him.

Dorothy, Men Behaving Badly

– How about Darwin?
– Yes, Ross. I do want a son who'll be regularly beaten up in the schoolyard.

Ross Geller and Rachel Green, Friends

– Vicky?
– Icky with a 'v'.

Cosmo and Wanda, The Fairly Odd Parents

If it's a girl, Phoebe, naturally. And if it's a boy … Phoebo.

Phoebe Bouffau, Friends

– Sweet Pea is the worst name I've ever heard for a baby.
– What do you want me to call it? Baby Oyl?

Popeye and Olive Oyl, Popeye

I gave my kids normal names, not names like Peaches and Blossom, and Autumn and Apple and Cherry – like a range of Glade plug-ins.

Jack Dee

When I was introduced to a Texan businessman he looked aghast: 'Tarquin Olivier,' he said, 'now there's a name that smacks of overkill.'

Tarquin Olivier

Always end the name of your child with a vowel, so that when you yell, the name will carry.

Bill Cosby

I wanted to have children to continue the family name. Now I've got children, there are times when I beg them not to give their full name.

Rod Lake

Any child can tell you that the sole purpose of a middle name is so he can tell when he's in trouble.

Dennis Fakes

Donald Trump says he named his daughter Tiffany after his favourite store, Tiffany's. How ridiculous is that? I was saying so to my twins, Bargain and Booze.

Les Curtis

If you're gonna be a boxer, you gotta prepare for memory loss. So I named all my kids George. Including the girls.

George Foreman

Because of my father, from the ages of 7 to 15, I thought that my name was Jesus Christ and my brother, Russell, thought that his name was Dammit. 'Dammit, will you stop all that noise?' And, 'Jesus Christ, sit down!' One day, I'm out playing in the rain, and my father yelled, 'Dammit, will you get back in here!' I said, 'Dad, I'm Jesus Christ!'

Bill Cosby

My dad's so sweet. He named his first ulcer after me.

Ellie Firth

High Hopes

When my son was born, I had a dream that one day he might grow up to win a Nobel Prize. But I had another

dream that he might grow up to say, 'Do you want fries
with that?'

Robin Williams

My daughter was born under a lucky star. Lionel Blair had
the flat upstairs.

Bob Monkhouse

Dad had such high hopes for Vanessa and Corin but I was
the one of whom nothing was expected. I remember a
game the three of us played: Vanessa was the President of
the United States, Corin was the British Prime Minister –
and I was the royal dog.

Lynn Redgrave

When you become a parent, it is your biggest chance to
grow again. You have another crack at yourself.

Fred Rogers

May you build a ladder to the stars and climb on every
rung.

Bob Dylan

Bringing up Baby

Child-Rearing Myth Number One: labour ends when the
child is born.

Rod Lake

Apparently, you have to get up during the night
occasionally. Don't know why. I haven't read the book yet.

Gary, Men Behaving Badly

Fathers' Wit

I'm 484 months old. Can you tell I'm a new father?

Reno Goodale

I used to think that having a dog was adequate preparation for parenthood, but I'm told they're not exactly the same, pet ownership and child rearing.

Paul Reiser

A baby is an alimentary canal with a loud voice at one end and no sense of responsibility at the other.

Ronald Knox

A baby is the most complicated object made by unskilled labour.

Steven Wright

Babies are the enemies of the human race.

Isaac Asimov

My first husband, The World's Best Father, was so horrified by the advent of fatherhood that he went out and had a vasectomy as soon as the clinic opened on Monday morning.

Julie Burchill, ex-Mrs Tony Parsons

Parenting remains the greatest single preserve of the amateur.

Alvin Toffler

Have you any idea how difficult it is to be a father? Children forget that although they have no previous experience of being children, their fathers have no previous experience of being fathers.

Peter Ustinov

The toughest job in the world isn't being a President. It's being a parent.

Bill Clinton

There are no perfect parents. Even Jesus had a distant real father and a domineering mother.

Bob Smith

When I wake up in the morning, I think of *me* first and then my wife and then my children. I'd like to meet the guy that can honestly admit he does differently.

Jerry Lewis

Parenting Class? That's supposed to come natural. It'd be like taking a Smelling Class.

Raymond Barone, Everybody Loves Raymond

Raising kids is part joy and part guerrilla warfare.

Ed Asner

You want to bring up Chloe? You couldn't bring up phlegm!

Sonia Jackson, EastEnders

Arnold Schwarzenegger's future mother-in-law gave him a Labrador as an engagement present. She told her daughter to watch the way he treated the dog because one day that's the way he would treat his kids. A couple of years later, he ran over the dog.

Jack Dee, Have I Got News For You

The most extraordinary thing about having a child is that people think I'm a responsible human being.

Colin Farrell

Fathers' Wit

People often ask me, 'What's the difference between couplehood and babyhood?' In a word? Moisture. Everything in my life is now more moist. Between your spittle, your diapers, your spit-up and drool, you got your baby food, your wipes, your formula, your leaky bottles, sweaty baby backs, and numerous other untraceable sources – all creating an ever-present moistness in my life, which heretofore was mainly dry.

Paul Reiser

I'm terrified of raising a kid. I can't even keep my plants alive.

Bill Maher

All children alarm their parents, if only because you are forever expecting to encounter yourself.

Gore Vidal

Don't worry, the first 40 years are the worst.

Cliff Jackson

The toughest part of parenthood has nothing to do with putting food on the table, clothes in the closet, or tuition money in the bank. The toughest part of parenthood is never knowing if you're doing the right thing.

D. L. Stewart

Trust yourself. You know more than you think you do ... What good mothers and fathers instinctively feel like doing for their babies is the best of all.

Dr Benjamin Spock

When I first picked up my little girl, I was terrified her head would drop off.

Alan Read

Bringing up Baby

If you pull at babies too hard, they'll spew like a can of beer. I used to shake up my daughter, hand her to people I didn't like and say, 'Would ya mind holding her a minute?'

Jeff Foxworthy

Child-rearing advice: Try to get one that doesn't spit up. Other than that, you're on your own.

Calvin Trillin

Raising a child today is a journey so fraught with bad directions, backseat drivers, and contradicting maps, that it's a wonder we even make it out of the maternity hospital parking garage.

Dennis Miller

Nothing gets you ready for that first night when you're out of the hospital and alone, and she's crying and won't stop and you're holding her against you while her screams rock your chest.

Bob Greene

Ever since the baby's been born, I find I cannot take my eyes off her. Instead of television, I now watch her and it's the best show I've ever seen.

Dave Bernard

A baby first laughs at the age of four weeks. By that time their eyes focus well enough to see you clearly.

Dr Jonathan Agnew

Next time you're at the park, take a look at the new parents. At first they may appear to be basking in their new-found parental bliss. But look closer. See that facial twitch? That's no twitch, my friend. That man's a hostage and he's trying to blink you a message.

Ray Romano

Fathers' Wit

The questions new dads care most about are: Will I ever have sex again? How are we going to pay for all this stuff? Will I be like my father – and is that good or bad?

Bradley Richardson

I realize I'm succumbing to the occupational disease, the father-jitters or new-parenthood-shakes, expressed in, 'Hark, the child's screaming, she must be dying.' Or, 'She's so quiet, d'you think she's dead?'

Laurie Lee

I've become a baby bore. In a week I have done the following: bought a roof rack; discovered myself to have an opinion on the hydroscopic capabilities of Pampers; thought about going to IKEA; bought a house because of its garden and proximity to a reputable junior school; heard myself complaining about violence on television; started reading the nutritional-value information on the back of rusk packets.

John Diamond

My God, the nursery still looks like little more than a store room! I spoke to my husband, and he suggested that we paper it with bills from the hospital. I thought it was rather tasteless and said as much. The baby is a girl and the hospital bills are blue.

Julie Walters

There are 152 distinctly different ways of holding a baby – and all are right.

Heywood Broun

Things a father should know: how to prise his wife's hands from the neck of their firstborn and clasp them round a glass of gin.

Katharine Whitehorn

Bringing up Baby

Taking care of a newborn baby means devoting yourself, body and soul, 24 hours a day, seven days a week, to the welfare of someone whose major response, in the way of positive reinforcement, is to throw up on you.

Dave Barry

Did you know babies are nauseated by the smell of a clean shirt?

Jeff Foxworthy

Babies are more self-obsessed than a supermodel on angel dust. Are they mad? They look mad. They spend an awful lot of time pointing at nothing. Their only ambition seems to be to make appalling smells.

David Quantick

If you were to open up a baby's head – and I'm not for a moment suggesting that you should – you would find nothing but an enormous drool gland.

Dave Barry

Looking after a baby is child's play! I mean, who else stops crying just by sticking a dummy in their mouth?

Carl Whitehouse

Despite the fact you have done nothing these nine months, the baby is 50 per cent you. Some mothers never forgive the father for this.

Marcus Berkmann, Fatherhood: The Truth

The worst feature of a new baby is its mother's singing.

Kin Hubbard

Fathers' Wit

- Yeah, sure, for you, a baby's all fun and games. For me, it's diaper changes and midnight feedings.
- Doesn't Mom do all that stuff?
- Yeah, but I have to hear about it.

Homer and Lisa Simpson

I never left Gloria alone when she was a baby. Wherever I went, I made sure her mother was with her.

Archie Bunker, All in the Family

- The doctor said that after you'd had the baby, you might feel that life wasn't worth living.
- I've felt that way for a long time, Frank.

Frank and Bette Spencer, Some Mothers Do 'Ave 'Em

Things a father should know: that Elizabethandthechildren is actually four words, not one.

Katharine Whitehorn

Kids. They're not easy. But there has to be some penalty for sex.

Bill Maher

I used to walk into a party and scan the room for attractive women. Now I look for women to hold my baby so I can eat potato salad sitting down.

Paul Reiser

A baby is an inestimable blessing and bother.

Mark Twain

My friend has a baby boy. I'm recording all the noises he makes so later I can ask him what he meant.

Steven Wright

Bringing up Baby

Once you have a kid you'll never win another argument with your wife, because in the game of marriage, giving birth is a royal flush. Nothing trumps motherhood.

Reno Goodale

The problem with men is that after the birth, we're irrelevant.

Dustin Hoffman

The reason your wife pays more attention to the baby than you is because the baby is a blood relation of your wife – he's her son. You're just some guy she met in a bar.

Garry Shandling

Heinz is coming out with a baby bottle shaped like a woman's breast. They should sell beer in it. They'd make a fortune.

Jay Leno

One of the reasons girls talk earlier than boys is breastfeeding. Boys would rather breastfeed than talk because they know they won't be getting that close again for another 15 years.

Paul Seaburn

I was in analysis for years because of a traumatic childhood: I was breastfed through falsies.

Woody Allen

Children are supposed to help hold a marriage together. They do this in a number of ways. For instance, they demand so much attention that a husband and wife, concentrating on their children, fail to notice each other's faults.

Richard Armour

Fathers' Wit

This is the Basic Baby Mood cycle, which all babies settle into once they get over being born:
MOOD ONE: Just about to cry.
MOOD TWO: Crying.
MOOD THREE: Just finished crying.

Dave Barry

When you're drawing up your list of life's miracles, you might place near the top the first moment your baby smiles at you.

Bob Greene

Whatever is on the floor will wind up in the baby's mouth. Whatever is in the baby's mouth will wind up on the floor.

Bruce Lansky

Actually what I've been surprised about in becoming a father is the lack of character that the baby has. It just lies there.

Guy Ritchie on baby Rocco

We have a baby now at our house. It's here all day long. And all night long. I don't know why they say you have a baby. The baby has you.

Gallagher

I'm not allowed to say 'hump' or 'screw' in front of the B-A-B-Y ... I just spelled the wrong word, didn't I?

Chandler Bing, Friends

Ever tried dressing a baby in a snowsuit? By the time you get it in there the snow's melted and it's spring.

Pete Geller

Obtain one large, unhappy live octopus. Stuff into a small net bag, making sure that all arms stay inside. Congratulations, you have passed the baby-dressing test.

Anon

Anyone who uses the phrase 'easy as taking candy from a baby' has never tried taking candy from a baby.

Roger Howe

A king, realizing his incompetence, can either delegate or abdicate his duties. A father can do neither. If only sons could see the paradox, they would understand the dilemma.

Marlene Dietrich

As a baby, I was almost perfectly spherical in shape, causing my parents frequent anxieties as they feared they had left me upside down, and forcing them to enter and re-enter rooms in which I had been left in order to check.

Peter Ustinov

My wife told me the baby had a runny nose. I asked if it was green or clean. We then had a 20-minute discussion about the boy's bodily fluids. It's like he's a tiny Bill Clinton.

Jimmy Cox, Rock Me Baby

That dear little baby tooth, with a small tag attached, reading: 'The first bicuspid that little Willie lost. Extracted from Daddy's hand on 5 April.'

W. C. Fields

For years parents have been buying books to document all the precious moments in their new baby's life – Baby's first tooth, first step, haircut. What have been ignored for too long are

Fathers' Wit

those 'alternative precious moments' that should be celebrated and remembered – like Baby's first projectile vomit; Baby's first tantrum in a crowded grocery store; Baby's 10,000th dirty diaper; Baby's first tattoo. Otherwise, you might forget them and think of becoming parents once again.

Jim Mullen, Baby's First Tattoo

Having children gives your life a purpose. Right now, my purpose is to get some sleep.

Reno Goodale

People who say they sleep like a baby usually don't have one.

Leo J. Burke

Why should I want a Society for the Prevention of Cruelty to Children to prosper, when there is a baby downstairs that kept me awake several hours last night with no pretext but a desire to make trouble?

Mark Twain

One parent or the other got up late in the night to come and see if your backside was moving up and down.

Garrison Keillor

Fill a small bag with 12 pounds of wet sand. At 8 p.m., begin to waltz and hum with the bag until 9 p.m. Lie down and get up again immediately. Sing every song you have ever heard. Fall asleep standing up, then make breakfast. Do this for five years. Look cheerful. Congratulations, you have now passed the baby night test.

Anon

We learn from experience. A man never wakes up his second baby just to see it smile.

Grace Williams

The baby wakes up in the wee wee hours of the morning.

Robert Robbins

A Father's Lot is Not a Nappy One

In the eyes of a mother, there is one single determining factor as to whether her husband is a good father or not: does he change the baby's nappy?

Anon

Changing diapers is such a symbol these days. And the focus is always on the man and whether or not he does it. But I don't see many self-help articles for new mothers on how to change the oil or mow the lawn.

Kevin Nelson

For every New Man changing nappies, there are 99 Newish Men dreaming about changing wives for one with a little less bounce around the bikini line.

Julie Burchill

Men can strip down an engine and put it back together, but changing a diaper? No way.

Brad Poole

The experts agree that mothers do not have a biological, psychological or natural advantage that automatically makes them better kiddie-caretakers than fathers. Clearly the experts have never watched a man change a diaper.

Michael Burkett

Fathers' Wit

Husbands are afraid to touch the child at first. The mother learns immediately that you can sling it over your shoulder and it will be just fine. My husband never changed a diaper; he was very proud of that. My child flew through the air; he'd say, 'She's wet' and toss her to me.

Joan Rivers

Any mother with half a skull knows that when Daddy's Little Boy becomes Mommy's Little Boy, the kid is so wet that he's treading water.

Erma Bombeck

A baby changes your dinner party conversation from politics to poop.

Maurice Johnson

It's important for husbands to know when to change a diaper. I figure every three days is about right.

Alan Thicke

If I'd waited for your dad to change you, you'd have worn the same diaper since you were 2.

Edith Bunker, All in the Family

Shouldn't there ought to be some kinda relationship between how much a baby eats and what comes out the other end? It's like that tiny clown car at the circus and all the clowns keep on coming out and out and out.

Dennis Miller

'Diaper' backwards spells 'repaid'. Think about it.

Marshall McLuhan

Changing nappies is something that men are instinctively nauseated by, and it is natural to leave that to the mothers.

Dr Cohen-Salal

A Father's Lot is Not a Nappy One

My friend's baby had an accident in its diaper. The mother comes over and says, 'Oh, how adorable. Brandon made a gift for Daddy.' I'm thinking this guy must be real easy to shop for on Father's Day.

Garry Shandling

It should be stressed that the muscle-bound Adonises you see on posters and cards in tender poses with young infants are not the real fathers of the children. No one with a new baby has the energy to pump iron for two hours a day. Moreover, you should never hold a naked baby boy up in front of you because he will urinate in your face.

Jeremy Hardy

The first time you change your son's diaper and he pees all over you is not an accident. It's foreshadowing.

Esquire *magazine*

Never change diapers in mid stream.

Don Marquis

Men who fought in the world's bloodiest of wars are apt to faint at the sight of a truly foul diaper.

Gary Christenson

The first time you deal with a nappy full of impacted crap, it is a life-altering encounter. Your emotions when you come face to face with it are something you could never anticipate, unless you work in a hospital or on a pig farm.

Charles Jennings

When it comes to changing diapers there's only one thing to remember: never scratch and sniff.

David Letterman

Fathers' Wit

Baby caca is like Kryptonite to a father. The dog's looking at you going, 'You don't rub *his* face in it.'

Robin Williams

After a while of changing diapers you learn to hold your breath like a Hokkaido pearl diver.

Dennis Miller

Changing nappies brings you into close contact with every digestive quirk … You will discover what babies can digest and what they can't. Sweet corn and raisins will never seem the same again, and the seed distribution systems of tomatoes will become instantly clear to you.

Michael Rosen

Things a father should know: how to change a nappy – *and* dispose of the old one.

Katharine Whitehorn

I once knew a chap who had a system of just hanging the baby on the clothes line to dry and he was greatly admired by his fellow citizens for having discovered a wonderful innovation on changing a diaper.

Damon Runyon

Next time you're having a party and need some booze, don't go to the off-licence, go with your partner to the supermarket. Fill your trolley with booze, and booze alone … vodka, gin, tequila, wine, whatever. But just before you get to the checkout – put in a box of nappies. Then, when you get to the till and check everything through, pretend you don't have quite enough money – and put the nappies back. Whoever's on the till just looks at you like you're scum. It's brilliant.

Ed Byrne

Child-rearing

Kids are great. You can teach them to hate the things you hate and they practically raise themselves nowadays, you know, with the Internet and all.

Homer Simpson

How children survive being brought up amazes me.

Malcolm Forbes

There's so much crap talked about bringing up a child. A fucking moron could do it. Morons do bring up their children. It's just endless love, endless patience, that's it.

Bob Geldof

In the old days, of course, the Free World had an excellent system of high-quality, low-cost child care, namely your mother.

Dave Barry

Everybody knows how to raise children except the people who have them.

P. J. O'Rourke

All kids need is a little help, a little hope, and somebody who believes in them.

Earvin 'Magic' Johnson

I understand the importance of bondage between parent and child.

Dan Quayle

It seems to me that upbringings have themes. The parents set the theme, either explicitly or implicitly, and the children pick it up, sometimes accurately and sometimes

Fathers' Wit

not so accurately. The theme may be, for example, 'No matter what happens, we are fortunate to be together in this lovely corner of the earth,' or 'We have worked hard so that you can have the opportunities we didn't have.'

Calvin Trillin

The end product of child-raising is not the child but the parent.

Frank Pittman

Childhood is a time when kids prepare to become grown-ups, so to get them ready for the real world, I think it makes sense to totally traumatize your children.

George Carlin

I was in the garden with my 3-year-old daughter, Honey, who was blowing bubbles. The sun was shining, the birds were singing, she turned to me and said, 'Daddy, my life is bubbles.' I thought, how lovely, then I snatched the bubbles from her little hand and threw them away. Because you've gotta teach kids that life can be unfair. You've gotta teach kids the arbitrariness of existence.

Jonathan Ross

My parents raised me with the three magic words: total sensory deprivation.

Emo Philips

All I heard when I was growing up was, 'Why can't you be more like your cousin Sheila? Why can't you be more like your cousin Sheila?' Sheila died at birth.

Joan Rivers

When our son was about 18 months old, my wife got a book called *How to Teach Your Baby to Read*. Me, I was dubious. I thought it was better to teach our child not to pull boogers out of his nose and hand them to us as if they were party favours.

Dave Barry

I'd like to smack smug parents who say, 'Our 3-year-old's reading *Harry Potter*.' Well, my 3-year-old's smearing his shit on the fridge door.

Jack Dee

Teach your child to hold his tongue; he'll learn fast enough to speak.

Benjamin Franklin

It is no wonder people are so horrible when they started life as children.

Kingsley Amis

All women should know how to take care of children. Most of them will have a husband some day.

Franklin P. Jones

I love giving the kids a bath. There's great satisfaction in it. They get so dirty.

Curtis Black

A house is never perfectly furnished for enjoyment unless there is a child in it rising 3 years old, and a kitten rising 3 weeks old.

Robert Southey

There is a horrible idea, beginning with Rousseau, that natural man is naturally good. Anybody who's ever met a toddler knows this is nonsense.

P. J. O'Rourke

Fathers' Wit

The fundamental job of a toddler is to rule the universe.

Lawrence Kutner

A 2-year-old is like having a blender, but you don't have a top for it.

Jerry Seinfeld

Toddlers are crap. They're too big to pick up but too small to send to the shop for fags.

Jeff Green

A philosopher told me that, having examined the civil and political order of societies, he now studied nothing except the savages in the books of explorers, and children in everyday life.

Nicolas Chamfort

There's only two things a child will share willingly – communicable diseases and his mother's age.

Dr Benjamin Spock

A child is a curly, dimpled lunatic.

Ralph Waldo Emerson

After a long day caring for our three kids, my wife had reached the end of her tether. She was teary and cranky. My son said, 'Daddy, is she teething?'

Craig Ackland

Adam and Eve had many advantages, but the principal one was that they escaped teething.

Mark Twain

The quickest way for a parent to get a child's attention is to sit down and look comfortable.

Lane Olinghouse

A child of 3 cannot raise its chubby fist to its mouth to remove a piece of carpet which it is through eating, without being made the subject of a psychological seminar of child-welfare experts.

Robert Benchley

For toddlers I suggest leaving their mittens on year-round, indoors and out. That way they can't get into aspirin bottles, liquor cabinets or boxes of kitchen matches. Also, it keeps their little hands clean for mealtimes.

P. J. O'Rourke

Kids do say the darndest things, but that's once in a blue moon, and in between it's a lot of drivel.

Bill Maher

He uses my body for nine months like it's an all-you-can-eat salad bar and his first word is, 'Dada.'

Beth Cox, Rock Me Baby

I'm guessing Brooklyn Beckham's first words were Gucci, Gucci, goo.

Polly Stone

I grew up in a political family. The first words I spoke as a child were Mommy, Daddy, and Constituency.

Pat Robertson

A Brief Guide to Baby-talk: Takes after his father: *Snores and suffers from wind*; No trouble at all: *We have a nanny*; Loves books: *Sucks them*; Advanced for his age: *Likes a drop of gin in his milk*; Loveable: *Fat*.

John Koski and Mitchell Symons

Fathers' Wit

The most popular question for small children is 'Why?'
They can use it anywhere and it's usually impossible to
answer:
CHILD: What's that?
YOU: It's a goat.
CHILD: Why?

Dave Barry

If a kid asks where rain comes from, I think a cute thing to
tell them is, 'God is crying.' And if they ask why God is
crying, another cute thing to tell them is, 'Probably because
of something you did.'

Jack Handey

My kid's endless questions are driving me crazy … why,
why, why? Why didn't I pull out?

Steve McGrew

Children seldom misquote you. They more often repeat
word for word what you shouldn't have said.

Mae Maloo

We had my boss and his wife over for dinner and my
4-year-old insisted on saying goodnight. As my boss's
wife was patting him on the head, he said, 'My daddy
wears Homer Simpson pants and farts in bed.' Bye bye
promotion.

Mitch Goldberg

– How you doin'?
– How you doin'?
– Do you like hockey?
– Do you like hockey?
– This is a very important game.
– This is a very important game.

– Cut the crap, kid.
– Cut the crap, kid.
– How much wood could a woodchuck chuck if a
  woodchuck could chuck wood? Yeah, I thought so!

Sonny Koufax and adopted son, Julian, Big Daddy

Why is it that when you let a 3-year-old dress herself,
she always dresses like an East European prostitute – pink
tights, pink dress, pink shoes, little plaits and bright red
lipstick?

David Baddiel

How to throw a children's party: dig a pit, throw in the
kids and ice cream, add chocolate sauce; an hour later take
out and send home.

Tony Kornheiser

In stark contrast to grown-up parties, partygoers at
children's parties don't become embarrassingly drunk. It is
the birthday-boy's or girl's father who becomes
embarrassingly drunk.

Jeremy Hardy

Any child's birthday party in which the number of guests
exceeds the number of the actual age of the child for
whom the party is being given will end in disaster.

Pierre Burton

Hosting your child's party is like an exercise in riot control.
Suddenly you find yourself spotting the ring leaders,
appealing to the more moderate children to try and keep
order, abandoning the living room to the mob and trying to
consolidate your power base in the kitchen.

Jeremy Hardy

Fathers' Wit

I have just returned from a children's party. I am one of the few survivors.

Percy French

– He's more like his father every day.
– He sure is. This morning he was playing with a corkscrew.

Nora Charles and Stella, Shadow of the Thin Man

To our parents, we seem always to be works-in-progress.

Frank Pittman

As soon as I stepped out of my mother's womb on to dry land, I realized that I had made a mistake – that I shouldn't have come; but the trouble with children is that they are not returnable.

Quentin Crisp

Parents are the bones upon which children sharpen their teeth.

Peter Ustinov

Don't try to make your children grow up to be like you or they may do it.

Russell Baker

If you cannot open a childproof bottle, use pliers or ask a child.

Bruce Lansky

My parents never wanted me to get upset about anything. They couldn't tell me when a pet had died. One day I woke up and my goldfish had gone. I said, 'Where's Fluffy?' They said, 'He ran away.'

Rita Rudner

I try to raise my kids to be generous and sharing. The other day, my 3-year-old daughter offered me her bag of sweets and said, 'Take a lot. Take two.'

Edward Price

Closely he cuddled up to me,
And put his hand in mine,
Till all at once I seemed to be
Afloat on seas of brine.
Sabean odours clogged the air
And filled my soul with dread,
Yet I could only grin and bear
When Willie wet the bed.

Eugene Field

The child was a keen bed-wetter.

Noël Coward

I found this priceless piece of advice in a childcare book dated 1595: 'A mouse roasted and given to children to eat remedieth pissing the bed.' So now you know.

Reg Collins

If you wonder where your child left his roller skates, try walking around the house in the dark.

Leopold Fechtner

Have you seen those toilet-training books? There's the popular, *Everybody Poops*; or the less popular, *Nobody Poops But You*; or, for Catholics, *You're a Naughty, Naughty Boy and That's Concentrated Evil Coming Out of Your Bottom*.

Peter Griffin, Family Guy

Training children is mostly a matter of pot luck.

Bob Monkhouse

Fathers' Wit

I was watching *Peter Pan* with my 6-year-old daughter and she says, 'Daddy, how does Captain Hook wipe his bottom?' I just said, 'Smee does it.'

Bob Saget

I loved those years of being Mr Mom. One of the saddest days in my life was when Jennifer said, 'Dad, I can wash my own hair.'

Billy Crystal

– Dad, look at me.
– But if I pay attention to you, I have to stop watching TV. You can see the bind I'm in.

Bart and Homer Simpson

By the age of 6, the average child will have completed the basic American education. From television, the child will have learned how to pick a lock, commit a fairly elaborate hold-up, prevent wetness all day long, get the laundry twice as white, and kill people with a variety of sophisticated armaments.

Anon

When I was a kid, I would ask my dad if I could watch TV and he'd always say, 'Yes, but don't turn it on.'

Fragger, b3ta.com

Try treating your dog the way America treats its kids. Give the puppy her own set of house keys and put her in front of the television instead of taking her for a walk. Let her eat anything she wants and house train herself. Send her to another master for visitation at the weekends. And when she comes into heat, turn her loose in the pound.

P. J. O'Rourke

Parents exist to be grown out of.

John Wolfenden

Being a father is harder than being a rock 'n' roll singer on the road because any second your kid will run through the door with a 16-inch nail sticking through his head, going, 'Daddy, daddy, I just got hit by a 4x2.'

Ozzy Osbourne

The myriad disasters I envisaged for my own children in early life, such as contact with runaway juggernauts, rabid squirrels or molesting adults, were by some miracle successfully bypassed.

Robert Morley

The worst thing that can happen to a man is to have his wife come home and he has lost the child. 'How did everything go?' 'Just great, we're playing hide and seek and she's winning.'

Sinbad

My son Lawrie ran to me in tears. 'What's wrong?' I said. 'I stubbed my toe,' he wept. I took a closer look and asked which one hurt. Lawrie said, 'The one that ate roast beef.'

David Best

Being a father is the hardest job in the world. You try to lead your kids up the right path, but who am I to lead anybody up any fucking path? How can I give out the rules when I'm worse than them most of the time? When you see me coming home in police cars, in fucking ambulances, in straitjackets and chains?

Ozzy Osbourne

Fathers' Wit

The essential skill of parenting is making up answers. When an experienced father is driving down the road and his kid asks how much a certain building weighs, he doesn't hesitate for a second. '3,457 tons,' he says.

Dave Barry

Son, I don't want you to do that because I don't want Mom to worry, all right? When she worries she starts saying things like, 'I told you so,' or 'Stop doing that, I'm asleep.'

Peter Griffin, Family Guy

A bathroom is a place where your child doesn't need to go until you're backing your car out of the driveway.

Anon

What it really means to be a parent is: you will spend an enormous portion of your time lurking outside public-toilet stalls. Children almost never have to go to the bathroom when they are within a few miles of their own home toilets. Then, when you get where they're going, let's say a restaurant, the child will wait until your entrées arrive, then announce that they have to go. If it is an especially loathsome bathroom that has not been cleaned since the fall of Rome, the child will immediately announce that they have to do a Number Two.

Dave Barry

In the end the negative aspects of being a parent – the loss of intimacy, the expense, the total lack of free time, the incredible responsibility, etc. – are more than outweighed by the positive aspects, such as never again lacking for primitive drawings to attach to your refrigerator with magnets.

Dave Barry

Child-rearing

I bought a beautiful new fridge with a stainless steel door. It came with a spray so that children's paintings won't stick to it. Because you don't want it ruined, do you? 'That's nothing like a rocket, that.' Still, you have to compromise. The kids wanted fridge magnets. I said, 'Okay, but only one, and I choose.' I chose a life-size picture of a fridge door.

Jack Dee

Infants need the most sleep, and, what is more, get it. Stunning them with a soft, padded hammer is the best way to ensure their getting it at the right times.

Robert Benchley

If your child refuses to go to sleep, try acting out a nursery rhyme – Rockabye Baby always works for me.

David Letterman

I was reading Bible stories to my young son at bedtime … 'The man named Lot was warned to take his wife and flee out of the city but his wife looked back and was turned to salt.' My son sat up suddenly and said, 'What happened to the flea?'

Jason Wilson

My father's sonorous voice brought Kipling's 'great grey-green, greasy Limpopo River all set about with fever-trees' snaking right to the foot of my bed.

Victoria Secunda

– Daddy, tell me a story.
– Life stinks, The End.

Robbie and Earl Sinclair, Dinosaur

When I was a kid, I used to imagine animals running under my bed. I told my dad, and he solved the problem quickly. He cut the legs off my bed.

Lou Brock

Fathers' Wit

[*Eric is tucking his young sons into bed*]
ERIC CAMDEN: I love you guys.
SAM CAMDEN: I love Spiderman.
DAVID CAMDEN: I love Batman.
ERIC CAMDEN: I love Batman too.
SAM CAMDEN: What about Spiderman?
ERIC CAMDEN: I love him too. Good night boys. [to himself]
               That was the best conversation I had all day.

Seventh Heaven

Never let a child wearing Superman pyjamas sleep on the top bunk.

Anon

Always kiss your children goodnight – even if they're already asleep.

H. Jackson Brown Jr

Will I Ever Have Sex Again?

– Could you knock before entering our bedroom?
– Like I'm gonna walk in on anything …

Kerry and Paul Hennessy, 8 Simple Rules for Dating
My Teenage Daughter

Children always assume the sexual lives of their parents come to a grinding halt at their conception.

Alan Bennett

I haven't had sex since Dorothy got pregnant. That's four months. I could do it with that bar stool right now. It wouldn't take long … Dorothy and I tried to have sex a month or so ago, but it was like trying to mount a giant, pink turtle.

Gary, Men Behaving Badly

Will I Ever Have Sex Again?

– Having sex with a pregnant woman is like putting gas in a car you just wrecked.
– Well, luckily Peggy pulls into self-service.

Jefferson and Al Bundy, Married … With Children

Sex during pregnancy – sometimes the foetus joined in and jived about a bit, so it was like doing it with someone else in the room.

Michael Rosen

I could have been sexually abused, but after I was born my parents were hardly interested in having sex with each other.

P. J. O'Rourke

After you've had children sex slows down. We have sex every three months now. Every time I have sex, the next day, I pay my quarterly taxes. Unless it's oral sex, then I renew my driver's licence.

Ray Romano

I've learned that as a parent, when you have sex, your body emits a hormone that drifts down the hall into your child's room and makes them want a drink of water.

Jeff Foxworthy

My mother said the best time to ask my dad for anything was when he was having sex. Not the best advice I've ever been given.

Jimmy Carr

When I caught my parents having sex, my dad looked at me and just said one thing: 'It's more fun than it looks.'

Eric Foreman, That 70s Show

I could never take condoms seriously after the experience as a toddler of finding one of Daddy's special balloons under my parents' bed and taking it in turns with a small friend to blow it up. I never was taken with the smell of hot rubber, anyway.

Julie Walters

Fathers and Family Life

Now remember. As far as anyone knows, we're a nice normal family.

Homer Simpson

Every family has a secret, and the secret is that it's not like other families.

Alan Bennett

I have never understood this liking for war. It panders to instincts already well catered for in any respectable domestic establishment.

Alan Bennett

The family – that dear octopus from whose tentacles we never quite escape, nor, in our innermost hearts, ever quite wish to.

Dodie Smith

Father, Mother, and Me,
Sister and Auntie say
All the people like us are We,
And everyone else is They.

Rudyard Kipling

Fathers and Family Life

A family is a social unit where the father is concerned with parking space, the children with outer space, and the mother with closet space.

Evan Esar

A family is a group of people who each like different breakfast cereal.

Milton Berle

Where does the family start? It starts with a young man falling in love with a girl – no superior alternative has yet been found.

Winston Churchill

A family is a unit composed not only of children but of men, women, an occasional animal, and the common cold.

Ogden Nash

Apparently, one in five people in the world are Chinese. And there are five people in my family, so it must be one of them. It's either my mum or my dad. Or my older brother, Colin. Or my younger brother, Ho-Cha-Chu. But I think it's Colin.

Tommy Cooper

Fathers should be neither seen nor heard. That is the only proper basis for family life.

Oscar Wilde

The place of the father in the modern suburban family is a very small one, particularly if he plays golf.

Bertrand Russell

Having a family is like having a bowling alley installed in your brain.

Martin Mull

Fathers' Wit

I've been married twice, the first producing two boys, the second time introducing me to two stepdaughters and then producing a boy of our own. This 'blended family' gives rise to the complaint by one of us: 'Your children are fighting my children and our child started it.'

Michael Rosen

From the teenager's perspective, remarriage can feel like a hostile takeover.

Laurence Steinberg

My parents have been divorced three times. Ours wasn't so much a broken home as a derelict one. When he left, my dad said, 'You're the head of the family now. Look after your mum and sisters.' What did he expect me to do? Pick my mum up from work on my Chopper bike?

Jeff Green

Family values? I'm sick of hearing about them. The reason most people are in therapy is because of their families.

Judy Carter

I believe that more unhappiness comes from this source than from any other – the attempt to prolong family connections unduly and to make people hang together artificially who would never naturally do so.

Samuel Butler

When I can no longer bear to think of the victims of broken homes, I begin to think of the victims of intact ones.

Peter de Vries

I come from a rough and ready family. Father was always rough, and mother was always ready.

Sid Snot, The Kenny Everett Show

Fathers and Family Life

All the men in my family were bearded, and most of the women.

W. C. Fields

Our family didn't exactly come from the wrong side of the tracks, but we were certainly always within the sound of the train whistles.

Ronald Reagan

I think a dysfunctional family is any family with more than one person in it.

Mary Karr

Govern a family as you would cook a small fish – very gently.

Chinese proverb

The great gift of family life is to be intimately acquainted with people you might never even introduce yourself to had life not done it for you.

Kendall Hailey

If you can't get rid of the family skeleton, you may as well make it dance.

George Bernard Shaw

Heredity is what sets the parents of a teenager wondering about each other.

Laurence J. Peter

I hate family reunions. Family reunions are those times when you come face to face with your family tree and realize some branches need to be cut.

René Hicks

It takes about five years for a walnut tree to produce nuts, but this is not true of a family tree.

Louie Wilson

Fathers' Wit

You're probably a redneck if your family tree doesn't fork.

Jeff Foxworthy

She's descended from a long line that her mother was once silly enough to listen to.

Gypsy Rose Lee

I don't know who my grandfather was; I am much more concerned to know what his grandson will be.

Abraham Lincoln

A Hollywood aristocrat is anyone who can trace his ancestry back to his father.

Jay Leno

Ashes to ashes and clay to clay; if the enemy don't get you, your own folk may.

James Thurber

Blood is thicker than water and much more difficult to get out of the carpet.

Woody Allen

My sister is my mum, my dad is my granddad and my uncle is my dad.

Zoe Slater, EastEnders

Freud is a lot of nonsense. The secret of all neurosis is to be found in the family battle of wills to see who can refuse longest to help with the dishes.

Julian Mitchell

Everybody wants to save the earth. Nobody wants to help Mom do the dishes.

P. J. O'Rourke

Fathers and Family Life

I have learned that my kids, like most kids, would rather work all night long in a salt mine than rake leaves at home.

Phil Donahue

Any child who is anxious to mow the lawn is too young to do it.

Bob Phillips

Any kid will run any errand for you if you ask at bedtime.

Red Skelton

There are three ways to get something done: do it yourself, hire someone, or forbid your kids to do it.

Rick Davies

My kids learn how to operate a computer but never learn how to use a clothes hanger.

Andy Tate

When I was a boy, my family took great care with our snapshots. We posed in front of expensive cars, homes that weren't ours. We borrowed dogs. Almost every family picture taken of us when I was young had a different borrowed dog in it.

Richard Avedon

My family is really boring. They have a coffee table book called *Pictures We Took Just to Use up the Rest of the Film.*

Penelope Lombard

You take the people you love pretty much the way you find them. Their worst qualities are often linked with their best ones.

Benjamin Cheever

Fathers' Wit

If you want to find out what your family thinks of you, die broke, and see who comes to your funeral.

Gregory Nunn

This book is dedicated to my mother, Mrs Frieda Seidman; to my daughters, Laurie Jo and Mona Helene; and to my wife Sylvia. All equally dear to me, but for safety's sake listed here alphabetically according to first name.

Gerald Lieberman

Have you ever had one of those days when you have had to murder a loved one because he is the devil?

Emo Philips

If murder had been allowed when dad was in his prime, our home would have been like the last act of *Othello* almost daily.

Nancy Mitford

If Mr Vincent Price were to be co-starred with Miss Bette Davis in a story by Mr Edgar Allan Poe directed by Mr Roger Corman, it would not fully express the pent-up violence and depravity of a single day in the life of the average family.

Quentin Crisp

There are families who live out their entire lives without a single thing of interest happening to them. I've always envied those families.

Tom Wingo, The Prince of Tides

A group of closely related persons living under one roof; it is a convenience, often a necessity, sometimes a pleasure, sometimes the reverse; but who first exalted it as admirable, an almost religious ideal?

Rose Macaulay

Fathers and Family Life

Home life as we understand it is no more natural to us than a cage is natural to a cockatoo.

George Bernard Shaw

Happy is said to be the family which can eat onions together. They are, for the time being, separate from the world, and have a harmony of aspiration.

Charles Dudley Warner

All well-regulated families set apart an hour every morning for tea and bread and butter.

Joseph Addison

The more keys a household owns, the more frequently will members of the family lock themselves out.

Freddie Johnson

Dad, Denise pushed us out of the bathroom and Rudy doesn't have all of the shampoo rinsed out of her hair so if she goes blind can we get a dog?

Vanessa Huxtable, The Cosby Show

– What have I said about comparing your sister to the Devil?
– That it's offensive to the Devil?

Red and Eric Foreman, That 70s Show

My 3-year-old son turned to his 5-year-old sister, and said, 'Just you wait till I'm older than you!'

Wayne Lowe

– Family dinners don't start until the whole family's here. Now, where's Daddy?
– He's getting seconds.

Alex Landis and Marlene Pellet, In-Laws

Fathers' Wit

Insanity is hereditary – you get it from your children.

Sam Levinson

Insanity runs in my family. It practically gallops.

Cary Grant

Just because your mother's nuttier than a Snickers bar doesn't mean that you should disrespect her.

Victor Pellet, In-Laws

I love being a dad, but the job is not without certain details that make me want to remove my clothes, climb City Hall, and do bird calls till I'm hauled off to some nice, safe place where I can't hurt myself.

Michael Burkett

They were a tense and peculiar family, the Oedipuses, weren't they?

Max Beerbohm

When I remember my family, I always remember their backs. They were always indignantly leaving places.

John Cheever

– But, Dad, why can't I go skiing with my friends? A lot of people I like are going to be there.
– Christmas is not about being with people you like. It's about being with your family.

Brad and Tim Taylor, Home Improvement

If God had meant Christmas to be a family occasion, he wouldn't have invented television, would he?

Rory McGrath

Fathers and Family Life

At Christmas time, my role is to eat the food, get drunk, and fall asleep in front of the telly wearing my novelty tie and cufflinks that double as spirit levels.

Tony Hawks

Every year it's the same ritual: Mum does the cooking, writes the cards, buys and wraps all the presents, puts up all the decorations, and Dad fuses the fairy lights.

Jeremy Slater

It is customarily said that Christmas is done for the kids – considering how awful Christmas is, and how little our society likes children, this must be true.

P. J. O'Rourke

I remember when I was about 6, a friend of mine said, 'There's no Father Christmas, you know.' And I said, 'Yes, there is, because last year he brought me lots of presents.' And my friend said, 'No, Father Christmas doesn't exist … it's your dad.' And I didn't know whether to be really upset or really excited – the fact that my dad, every Christmas, got into a sleigh and went round the whole world delivering presents to all the boys and girls.

Rory McGrath

Now, that just leaves little Maggie's Christmas present. Ah, a squeak toy. It says it's for dogs, but she can't read.

Homer Simpson

I bought my kids a set of batteries for Christmas with a note attached saying, 'Toys not included.'

Bernard Manning

Last Christmas, my son bought me a set of monogrammed handkerchiefs with the letter 'D' on them. I said, 'Why do they have "D" on them?' He said, 'They were in the sale.'

Rick Wakeman

Fathers' Wit

The important thing about Christmas is not the gifts. The important thing is having your family around resenting you.

Reno Goodale

Christmas is the time of year kids get toys their fathers can play with.

Milton Berle

I never know what to give my father for Christmas. I gave him $100 and said, 'Buy yourself something that will make your life easier.' So he went out and bought a present for my mother.

Rita Rudner

I think the real miracle of Christmas is how I get through it each year without killing my relatives.

Reno Goodale

There are only three occasions in Ireland when you'll find the whole family together: a wedding, a funeral, or if I've brought home a bag of chips.

Ardal O'Hanlon

Happiness is having a large, loving, caring, close-knit family in another city.

George Burns

The family you come from isn't as important as the family you're going to have.

Ring Lardner

I hate having workmen in. I don't like people in my house even when they're invited. The only reason I let the children stay is because it's the law, and the circus hasn't come through yet.

Jack Dee

Home is the place there's no place like.

Charles Schulz

Home is the place, when you have to go there, they have to take you in.

Robert Frost

Home is the wallpaper above the bed, the dinner table, church bells, bruised shins of the playground, the small fears that come with dusk.

Henry Grunwald

Size Matters

HOW BIG IS YOUR FAMILY?

Whenever I read newspaper stories about people who have, say, nine children, I never ask myself: 'How do they manage to take care of them all?' I ask myself: 'Where did they find the time to *conceive* them all?'

Dave Barry

I was the youngest of five boys. With so many brothers, my father bought us a dachshund so we could all pet him at the same time.

Bob Hope

The great advantage of living in a large family is that early lesson of life's essential unfairness.

Nancy Mitford

Fathers' Wit

I come from a large Irish Catholic family. Large Irish Catholic – it's redundant really.

John McGivern

I come from a large Jewish family: two children.

Karen Haber

I grew up with six brothers. That's how I learned to dance – waiting for the bathroom.

Bob Hope

– Dad, Denise is hogging the bathroom!
– Well, use the one downstairs!
– The small one? That's for guests!
– Well, pretend you don't live here!

Theo and Cliff Huxtable, The Cosby Show

Having one child makes you a parent; having two you are a referee.

David Frost

Anybody can have one kid. But going from one kid to two is like going from owning a dog to running a zoo.

P. J. O'Rourke

The child who is being raised strictly by the book is probably a first edition.

Aldous Huxley

How firstborns ever survive their parents' attention is beyond me. I tested the warmth of formulas from dusk to dawn, it seemed. We were so germ-conscious my wife even sterilized the skin of oranges before squeezing them.

Malcolm Forbes

When your first baby drops its dummy, you sterilize it.
When your second baby drops its dummy, you tell the dog
to 'Fetch!'

Bruce Lansky

Disconfect, *v.* What a parent does to sterilize a piece of
candy they dropped on the floor by blowing on it, assuming
this will somehow remove all the germs.

Anon

The first child is made of glass, the second porcelain, the
rest of rubber, steel and granite.

Richard Needham

For the first baby, we spent a big part of each day just
gazing at her.
For the second baby, we spent a big part of each day
watching to be sure our elder child wasn't squeezing or
hitting her.
For the third baby, we spent a big part of each day hiding
from the children.

Anon

For the first baby we colour-coordinated her in designer
clothes.
For the second baby we made sure her clothes were stain-
free.
For the third baby – boys can wear pink, can't they?

Anon

For the first baby, at the first sign of distress, we picked him up.
For the second baby, we picked him up when his wailing
threatened to wake our first-born.
For the third baby, we taught our 3-year-old how to rewind
the mechanical swing.

Anon

Fathers' Wit

For the first baby, when we left her with a babysitter, we called home five times.
For the second baby, we left a note for the babysitter saying where we could be reached.
For the third baby, we left instructions for the babysitter to call only if she saw blood.

Anon

The beauty of 'spacing' children many years apart lies in the fact that you have time to learn the mistakes that were made with the older ones – which permits you to make exactly the opposite mistakes with the younger ones.

Sydney Harris

I got more children than I can rightly take care of, but I ain't got more than I can love.

Ossie Guffy

It doesn't matter how many kids you have. Like work, a kid expands to fill the time available. One or six – they'll take up 100 per cent of your time.

Max Erhardt

When you're the only pea in the pod, your parents are likely to get you confused with the Hope Diamond.

Russell Baker

Children are like pancakes: you should always throw out the first one.

Peter Benchley

I'm an only child, although I did have an imaginary friend – who my parents actually preferred.

Chandler Bing, Friends

Jesus was an only child, and thank God, because who would want to be Jerry, the brother of Christ? 'Hi, I'm Jerry, the plumber in the family. No, I don't do the miracles.'

Robin Williams

The question that's probably uppermost in the child's mind is: why do my parents want to have a baby? Don't they love me? And if they love me, why do they need another one? Aren't I enough? Imagine for a minute yourself in a similar situation. Your husband comes home and says: 'Honey, I love you so much, I've decided to go get another wife so I can have two.' How would you feel?

Lawrence Balter

When I was a kid, we had a quicksand pit in our backyard. I was an only child … eventually.

Steven Wright

As a father of two there is a respectful question which I wish to ask of fathers of five: How do you happen to be still alive?

Ogden Nash

I've got two wonderful children – and two out of five ain't bad.

Henny Youngman

I have three children – one of each.

Rodney Dangerfield

After I'd been examined by the doctor, I couldn't wait to call my husband with the news. 'Can I call you right back, sweetheart,' he said, 'I'm on the john.' I suggested he stay seated for the news: 'We're having twins!' He promptly had the quickest, loosest bowel movement in history.

Jeanette Onorati

Fathers' Wit

When they showed me *two* 'little somethings' on the sonogram, the thought, 'twin boys' didn't pop into my head. For a second, I thought my son was going to make his living winning bar-bets.

Raymond Barone, Everybody Loves Raymond

Typical of Margaret. She produced twins and avoided the necessity of a second pregnancy.

Denis Thatcher

It is not economical to go to bed early to save the candles if the result is twins.

Chinese proverb

I have 2-year-old twins in my house, and it's nuts. I make excuses to get out. 'You need anything from anywhere? Anything from the Motor Vehicle Bureau? *Please!*'

Ray Romano

I remember the night me and my friends played Find the Lady by shuffling my infant triplets – only one of whom was female – on the sofa.

Richard Hannon

I grew up in a big family, six kids – seven, if you count my dad. He got all the attention, being the youngest.

Margaret Smith

My wife and I have five children and the reason why we have five children is because we do not want six.

Bill Cosby

Mum, Dad, Same Difference?

The difference between mums and dads is that mums work at work and work at home, and dads just go to work to work.

Jack, aged 8

Mothers are a biological necessity; fathers are a social invention.

Margaret Mead

If it were natural for fathers to care for their sons, they would not need so many laws commanding them to do so.

Phyllis Chesler

A woman knows everything about her children. She knows about dental appointments and football games and best friends and favourite foods and romances and secret fears and hopes and dreams. A man is vaguely aware of some short people living in the house.

Dave Barry

Men feel frazzled and angry if they have to answer three phone calls, and have a hard time settling back to work after the trauma. Women, on the other hand, tuck the phone in between their shoulders and their ears, hold a baby on one hip, stir a pot on the stove, all the while thinking about an idea for a story.

Barbara Grafton

Mothers wash dishes after every meal. Fathers wash dishes when the sink is so full that you have to go to the bathroom for a glass of water.

Michael Burkett

Fathers' Wit

A survey shows moms are better at baby talk than dads. Duh. For a dad, baby talk is, 'Here, you take him.'

Jay Leno

My mother taught me my ABCs. From my father I learned the glories of going to the bathroom outside.

Lewis Grizzard

A mother will go to the store for bread and milk, and return with enough groceries to feed Bangladesh for a year. A father will go to the store for bread and milk and return with bread, nacho-flavoured Doritos, and five dollars' worth of lottery tickets.

Michael Burkett

When my father is asked to do a job or something around the house he deliberately messes it up in the sure knowledge that my mother will stop him and say, 'Oh, forget it, I'll do it myself.'

Bob Hayden

My mum loves me as much as my dad does. But not so rough.

Jack, aged 5

If my father was the head of the house, my mother was its heart.

Huw, How Green Was My Valley

Father doesn't hear what Mother says, and Mother hears what Father does not say.

Carol Davies

My mother has gone to a woman's workshop on assertiveness training. Men aren't allowed. I asked my father what 'assertiveness training' is. He said, 'God knows, but whatever it is, it's bad news for me.'

Sue Townsend, The Secret Diary of Adrian Mole Aged 13¾

When he brings home the bacon she fries it. When she brings home the bacon they eat out.

Natasha Josefowitz

While Mom's Department includes every chore that involves fabric, tableaux and wainscoting, Dad's Department includes: Rodents of Unusual Size; Noise at Night Patrol; All Problems Relating to Utilities – gas vapours, septic tank miasma; Sharp Things That Move – jobs that include hedge clippers, lawn mowers, roto-tillers or any tool that has a whirring blade.

Sam Harper

You don't have to deserve your mother's love. You have to deserve your father's. He's more particular.

Robert Frost

It's clear that most American children suffer too much mother and too little father.

Gloria Steinem

Mothers curse. Fathers don't curse, they disinherit.

Irma Kurtz

The reason why mothers are more devoted to their children than fathers is that they suffer more in giving them birth and are more certain that they are their own.

Aristotle

My mother protected me from the world and my father threatened me with it.

Quentin Crisp

Fathers' Wit

The father is always a Republican towards his son, and his mother's always a Democrat.

Robert Frost

If a woman has to choose between catching a fly ball and saving an infant's life, she will choose to save the infant's life without even considering if there are men on base.

Dave Barry

My mother was like a drill sergeant. Dad was the commanding general.

George W. Bush

Mom never stopped talking and Dad never started. Even when he showed me how to pee, it was by example.

Michael Feldman

Some Great Things About Being a Dad

Anyone who hasn't had children doesn't know what life is.

Henry Miller

I don't need stuff like pot or booze. My high is my wife and kids.

Bill Cosby

Children are a great investment. They beat the hell out of stocks.

Peter Lynch

Some Great Things About Being a Dad

To show a child what once delighted you, to find the child's delight added to your own so that there is now a double delight seen in the glow of trust and affection, this is happiness.

J. B. Priestley

Children make you want to start life over.

Muhammad Ali

Kids are so easy to please. They get a kick out of sitting in the front seat of the car or getting the wishbone when we have roast chicken.

Al Brown

Children are a great comfort in your old age – and they help you to reach it faster.

Lionel Kauffman

Kids think the Christmas tree looks great no matter how lousy your decorating skills.

Alan Parry

If all the world thought and acted like children, we'd never have any trouble. The only pity is even kids have to grow up.

Walt Disney

Kids are great. They never know when I steal a few of their Smarties.

Wesley Smith

Having a kid is a great excuse to go to the garden centre and buy a Venus fly trap. And yes, feeding it flies does count as gardening.

Mick Rhodes

The great thing about having a kid is they never ask, 'Do these Huggies make my bum look big?'

Rod Lake

The great thing about kids is that they never get sick of beans on toast.

Graham Olson

Kids will go upstairs to fetch something you're too lazy to fetch yourself – just for the fun of the trip. Of course they never come back with the thing you actually wanted.

Paul Thompson

The thought of my sons carrying on after I'm gone is probably about as close to a belief in an afterlife as an ageing pagan like myself is likely to get. But curiously, it's close enough for comfort.

Carey Winfrey

Fathers Observed

– You did have a father?
– Oh, I'm sure I did. My mother was frugal in her habits, but she'd never economize unwisely.

Joe Orton, What the Butler Saw

My father was a man of great principle, though what those principles were I cannot say.

Eugene O'Neill

My father, driven by an immigrant spirit, with a sausage in one hand and the determination of a Rottweiler to sell it, became an American success story.

Ruby Wax

Fathers Observed

My father was a relentlessly self-improving boulangerie owner from Belgium with low-grade narcolepsy and a penchant for buggery. He would womanize, he would drink. He would make outrageous claims like he invented the question mark.

Dr Evil, Austin Powers

My dad was a kind of father figure to me.

Alan Coren

My father was a fastidious man. He dusted the chair on which the cat had been lying before occupying it himself. He ate a banana with a knife and fork.

Quentin Crisp

Derek Paine's father would eat a whole fried egg in a single mouthful; I never saw him do this, but Derek assured us of it one morning, making the point not boastfully but as though reserving a place for his father if the conversation became competitive.

Robert Robinson

My dad never did a thing around the house. He used to just sit in his chair threatening people. That was his job. Clipping people round the ear as they walked by, and saying, 'Just get on with something, will you?'

Jeff Green

My dad, Ozzy, is not the sort of dad who throws the ball around in the backyard and helps with the homework. Of course, I'm not that kind of kid, either. Mum always explained to us, 'That's just Daddy being crazy again.'

Kelly Osbourne

Fathers' Wit

My father had a profound influence on me – he was a lunatic.

Spike Milligan

A father who writes birthday greetings to his daughter on the inside of an unpeeled banana must be mentally disturbed. But he must also be quite ingenious. Yes, both.

Jostein Gaarder

Daddy Cool: How to Ride a Seesaw with Dignity, Wear a Donald Duck Hat with Style and Sing 'Bingo Was His Name-o'.

Richard Olivier, book title

Maybe someday I'll record a song I've written and dedicate it to my kids. It's called: 'You're the Reason I'm Not Cool Any More'.

Sinbad

It's a rule of fatherhood: A father will never seem 'cool' to his kids.

Ed Weston

My father hated radio and could not wait for television to be invented so that he could hate that too.

Peter de Vries

Mama Get a Hammer (There's a Fly on Papa's Head)

Country and Western song title

My father never escaped into heartiness: 'Hi, Bill! My son Biff has told me a lot about you,' and so on. No fellow human, however small, should be subjected to 'How do you like your school, Sonny?'

Wilfred Sheed

Austin Powers was born out of trying to celebrate my father's life. He loved to be silly. When I would bring friends home to play table hockey in the basement, if my dad didn't think they were funny, he wouldn't let them in the house.

Mike Myers

In the presence of the family my father would go into the hall to fart. My mother caught my eye once and said, 'He thinks no one can hear.'

Robert Robinson

The only lack of refinement I remember in my father was an unconscious habit he had, while reading his newspaper in his armchair, of picking his nose abstractedly and rolling the little bit of snot between his thumb and forefinger.

J. R. Ackerley

My father, like most Englishmen, could commit assault and battery with politeness.

Florence King

My father liked to collect yellow neckties and Yiddish curses. He never met a book he didn't finish.

Calvin Trillin

My father was a comic genius selling painted plastic signs that said things like 'Phil's Colour TV'. He would say to me, 'Sometimes I don't even care if I get the order, I just have to break the face.' He hated to see those serious businessman faces.

Jerry Seinfeld

– Are you of royal stock?
– No, my father was a grocer. I'm of vegetable stock.

Morecambe and Wise

Fathers' Wit

My father used to go round in some peculiar circles: he had one leg shorter than the other.

Rik Mayall

One day my father came running into the room waving a five-pound note, saying, 'Look what I got for you, son!' He'd sold me.

Ken Dodd

When my granddad passed away, my father told me by saying, 'All those with grandfathers, put up your hand,' then pointing at me and saying, 'Not so fast.'

Luxarama, b3ta.com

My father is a doctor, with the worst handwriting. He wrote me a note excusing me from gym class. I gave it to my teacher and she gave me all her money.

Rita Rudner

My father's a proctologist. My mother's an abstract artist. That's how I view the world.

Sandra Bernhardt

Mom and Pop were just a couple of kids when they got married. He was 18, she was 16 and I was 3.

Billie Holiday

My parents' marriage left me with two convictions: that human beings should not live together and that children should be taken from their parents at an early age.

Philip Larkin

By tonight my dad will be back in front of the TV in his beer-stained, flea-infested, duct-taped reclining chair, adjusting his shorts with one hand and cheering on Jean Claude Van Damme with the other.

Frasier Crane, Frasier

Fathers Observed

– Dad, your fly-hole's undone.
– Ah, the cage might be open but the beast's asleep.

Denise and Jim Royle, The Royle Family

The most terrifying aspect of Evelyn Waugh as a parent was that he reserved the right not just to deny affection to his children but to advertise an acute and unqualified dislike for them.

Auberon Waugh

My unhealthy affection for my second daughter has waned. I now despise all of my seven children equally.

Evelyn Waugh

My papa, Auberon Waugh, was wonderfully anarchic. You learned the anarchy from him, and you thought that was the way to be. So you went to school and were anarchic there and were flogged half to death – when all we were doing was emulating our father.

Alexander Waugh

Dad was just like Santa Claus and the Easter Bunny combined – just as charming – and just as fake.

Will Bloom, Big Fish

My mom was a ventriloquist and she was always throwing her voice. For ten years I thought the dog was telling me to kill my father.

Wendy Liebman

When I was little, my father used to make me stand in a closet for five minutes without moving. He said it was elevator practice.

Steven Wright

Fathers' Wit

When I was a kid I lost my parents on the beach. I asked a lifeguard to help me look for them. He said, 'I don't know, kid, there are so many places they could hide.'

Rodney Dangerfield

When I was young I used to think my family didn't like me. Because they used to send me to the store for bread, and then they'd move.

Richard Pryor

We used to have fire drill practice in my house. Everyone had their own special duty. My dad had to get the pets, my mom took the jewellery, my brother ran to get help. They told me to save the washer and dryer.

Ellen DeGeneres

When I was a kid, my father took me aside and left me there.

Ron Richards

If you have not had a good father, it is necessary to invent one.

Friedrich Nietzsche

Your father was Frankenstein, but your mother was the lightning.

Bela Lugosi, The Ghost of Frankenstein

Your mother was a hamster, and your father smelt of elderberries.

French Soldier, Monty Python and the Holy Grail

My father is Irish and my mother is Dutch. Which means my idea of a good time is to get drunk and drive my car into a windmill.

Kris McGaha

Fathers Observed

My mother is Welsh and my father is Hungarian. Which makes me well-hung.

Billy Riack

What is it George W. Bush says? If you ever get in a jam, call my dad – it's always worked for me.

David Letterman

My parents were very old world. Their values in life are God and carpeting.

Woody Allen

Daddy was one of those people who kept everything, old cigarette tins, magazines and especially the packaging that things had come in, 'in case they ever came in useful', which of course they never did. These days I suppose he would have collected all those Styrofoam moulds that come with radios and Magimixes.

Dame Edna Everage

I just got this telegram from daddy. Ten words exactly. After ten, it's extra. Daddy thinks of these things. If I had leprosy, there'd be a cable: 'Gee, kid, tough. Sincerely hope nose doesn't drop off. Love.'

Sally Bowles, Cabaret

My father could never have run a filling station. Giving free air, or even directions, would have left him apoplectic.

Richard Armour

Father preferred to begin a discussion by stating his conclusion and by calling yours nonsense, and to end the debate then and there.

Clarence Day

Fathers' Wit

I owe almost everything to my father and it's passionately interesting for me that the things that I learned in a small town, in a very modest home, are just the things that I believe have won the election.

Margaret Thatcher

I grew up thinking my parents knew everything. I'm sure they didn't, but at least they were smart enough to fake it. I don't even know how to do that yet.

Paul Reiser

Silent, austere, of high principle; ungentle of manner towards his children, but always a gentleman in his phrasing.

Mark Twain

When I was little, my father sang me 'Mairzy Doats'. He patiently held my head when a stomach virus made me vomit all night. He sewed button eyes on my teddy bear when its other eyes fell off.

Cynthia Heimel

He opened a jar of pickles when no one else could. He was the only one in the house who wasn't afraid to go into the basement by himself. It was understood when it rained, he got the car and brought it around to the door. When everyone was sick, he went out to get the prescription filled.

Erma Bombeck

My father was the best potato-masher one could wish for.

Hannah on Richard Nixon

One of the things Father specially detested about guests was the suddenness with which they arrived.

Clarence Day

– Dad, stop fiddling with yerself!
– I'm not fiddling with meself. I paid a quid for these
  underpants and I've got 50 pence worth stuck up me arse.

Denise and Jim Royle, The Royle Family

My father's boots went ahead. His boots were to me as unique
and familiar, as much an index to himself as his face was.

Alice Munro

Fathers don't wear bathing suits, they wear trunks. It's kind
of the same thing a tree would wear if it went swimming.

Jerry Seinfeld

When you're young, you think your dad's Superman. Then
you grow up and you realize he's just a regular guy who
wears a cape.

Dave Attell

My father was not a failure. After all, he was the father of
the President of the United States.

Harry S. Truman

What's it like to be the son of the President of the United
States? That's like asking a tomato how it feels to be red.

Ronald Reagan Jr

The worst misfortune that can happen to an ordinary man
is to have an extraordinary father.

Austin O'Malley

My father always wanted to be the corpse at every funeral,
the bride at every wedding and the baby at every
christening.

Alice Roosevelt Longworth, daughter of President Theodore Roosevelt

Fathers' Wit

My father, Aristotle Onassis, and Jacqueline Kennedy were well suited: he loved names and she loved money.

Alexander Onassis

My father, Groucho Marx, has shaken hands with Presidents, danced cheek to cheek with Marlene Dietrich, played baseball with Lou Gehrig, traded backhands with Jack Kramer, strummed guitar duets with the great Segovia, and he's insulted nearly everyone worth insulting.

Arthur Marx

That will do extremely well, child. You have delighted us long enough.

Mr Bennet, politely cutting short his daughter Mary's excruciating singing recital, Pride and Prejudice *by Jane Austen*

Children want to feel instinctively that their father is behind them as solid as a mountain, but, like a mountain, is something to look up to.

Dorothy Thompson

I think the saddest day of my life was when I realized I could beat my dad at most things, and Bart experienced that at the age of 4.

Homer Simpson

Mid-wife Crisis: any character in a Hollywood movie whose wife and/or kids are introduced more than an hour into the movie and who hugs and kisses any or all of them will be dead in the next 20 minutes (e.g. 'Goose' in *Top Gun*).

Edward Savio

Children begin by loving their parents. After a time they judge them. Rarely, if ever, do they forgive them.

Oscar Wilde

Fathers Observed

Parents are sometimes a bit of a disappointment to their children. They don't fulfil the promise of their early years.

Anthony Powell

– You should respect your parents. They won't be around for ever you know.
– Mine will. I'm going to have them stuffed. I might leave my dad's arm sticking out so I can use him as a tie rack.

Gary, Men Behaving Badly

We had political discussions around the dinner table. Once I said, 'Dad, what we need is an effective third political party.' He said, 'I'd settle for a second.'

Robin Philips

My dad used to purposefully provoke polemical arguments. He'd say things like – I mean, he never said actually this – but you'd be eating away and he'd go, 'Ah, y'know, that fella Hitler, he had a few good ideas.' The next minute, the place would erupt. He'd sit back and me and my two sisters would argue passionately that we didn't fucking believe it at all. That was the way we were. It was fairly explosive.

Bob Geldof

Your father wanted to shoot the Royal Family, abolish marriage, and put everybody who'd been to public school in a chain gang. Yeah, he was an idealist, your dad.

Mrs Dell, Morgan: A Suitable Case for Treatment

My dad can hit a century at cricket, catch a huge fish, remember the names of all the players in the England World Cup-winning soccer team, but he can never catch the 7.34 train.

Ted Amory

Fathers' Wit

Dad, who was the finest human being I have ever known, but who had the hairstyling skills and fashion flair of a lathe operator – cut my hair. This meant that I spent my critical junior high school years underneath what looked like the pelt of some very sick rodent.

Dave Barry

My dad adopted one of those Save the Children, and now he compares me to his adopted child. 'Why can't you be more like your sister, Keekee? Keekee dug an irrigation ditch for her entire village.'

Corey Kahane

If parents would only realize how they bore their children.

George Bernard Shaw

Something happens when a man reaches a certain age, that the news becomes the most important thing in his life. All fathers think one day they're going to get a call from the State Department. 'Listen, we've completely lost track of the situation in the Middle East. You've been watching the news. What do you think we should do?'

Jerry Seinfeld

I used to feel that all I ever did was take from my father: 'Dad, I need help building the shed.' 'Dad, can you lend me money for a car?' But now he has bought a computer, things are evening up quickly.

Den Schlaf

The longer I live the more keenly I feel that whatever was good enough for our fathers was not good enough for us.

Oscar Wilde

Fathers Observed

Nothing has a stronger influence psychologically on their environment, and especially on their children, than the unlived life of the parents.

Carl Jung

It is impossible to please the whole world and your father as well.

Jean de La Fontaine

My dad is waiting until he loses weight before buying new clothes. So he's still wearing his cub scout uniform.

Rita Rudner

My dad's trousers kept creeping up on him. By the time he was 65, he was just a pair of pants and a head.

Jeff Altman

I wouldn't say my father hated me, but at my christening, he tipped the vicar a fiver to hold me under.

Bob Monkhouse

My kids hate me. They keep leaving phone numbers of divorce lawyers in Mom's purse.

David Letterman

My kids hate me. Their three goldfishes are named 'We', 'Hate' and 'Dad.'

Herb Gold

If you have never been hated by your child, you have never been a parent.

Bette Davis

Be kind to your parents, though they don't deserve it; remember that 'grown-up' is a difficult stage of life.

Harold Rome

Fathers' Wit

Children despise their parents until the age of 40, when they suddenly become just like them – thus preserving the system.

Quentin Crewe

Just a little flash like the gesture of my hand in a conversation and *wham*, there's my old man. Right there, living inside me like a worm in the wood.

Sam Shepard

Sometimes being a father is like repossession. I'm possessed by the spirit of my late father. 'Don't do that!' All of a sudden, 'Oh, my God, I've turned into my dad.'

Robin Williams

Oh my God, I've turned into my father! I've been trying so hard not to become my mother, I didn't see this coming.

Rachel Green, Friends

If I turn into my parents, I'll either be an alcoholic blonde chasing 21-year-old boys, or I'll wind up like my mother.

Chandler Bing, Friends

I grew up to have my father's looks, my father's speech patterns, my father's posture, my father's opinions and my mother's contempt for my father.

Jules Feiffer

If our sons grow further away from us as the summers die one by one, our fathers grow even closer.

Tony Parsons

You think it's easy being a lousy father?

Nick Tortelli, Cheers

Fathers Observed

Some Rules for Being a Good Father: Never notice the whoopee cushion placed on your chair; Read out loud to your children; Never mock them; Leave child psychiatrists and writers of books to solve their own problems rather than yours.

Gyles Brandreth

To be a successful father there's one absolute rule: when you have a kid, don't look at it for the first two years.

Ernest Hemingway

A successful parent is one who raises a child so they can pay for their own psychoanalysis.

Nora Ephron

Before I married I had six theories about bringing up children, but no children; now I have six children and no theories.

John Wilmot

The rules for fathers are but three … Love, Limit, and Let Them Be.

Elaine M. Ward

Respect the child. Be not too much his parent. Trespass not on his solitude.

Ralph Waldo Emerson

The most important thing a father can do for his children is to love their mother.

Theodore Hesburgh

The first half of our lives is ruined by our parents and the second half by our children.

Clarence Darrow

Fathers' Wit

There's no pillow quite so soft as a father's strong shoulder.

Richard L. Evans

Nothing could get me if I was curled up on my father's lap, holding on to his ear with one thumb tucked into it. He had a big brown moustache and a wide Haldane nose with a small lump on it which I liked. When he kissed me it was rough and tickly. All about him was safe.

Naomi Mitchison

My parents have been there for me, ever since I was about 7.

David Beckham

I don't get why adopted kids want to trace their real fathers. Isn't it better to grow up thinking your dad's Neil Armstrong than find out he's Forrest Gump?

Drew Carey

– I won't have a mouse in the house. They're dirty, they carry disease, they eat garbage.
– So do the kids and you're not afraid of them.

Jill and Tim Taylor, Home Improvement

My mom has been nagging my father to take up a sport, so he took up bird-watching. He's very serious about it. He bought binoculars. And a bird.

Rita Rudner

My son has a new nickname for me. He calls me 'Baldy'. Son, I have a new word for you, 'Heredity'.

Dan Savage

The passing years make Junior wonder
Why Dad gets greyer and Mum gets blonder.

Anon

Fathers Observed

– You know, son, one day Mummy and Daddy will be old.
– Hmm, you're already old.
– I mean older.
– How much older can you get?

Ben and Michael Harper, My Family

My kids bring their friends over and say, 'We can tell how old our daddy is by counting the rings on his stomach.'

Tony Kornheiser

– I've decided to put an end to this madness that's ruining all our lives.
– Mum, you mean you're going to kill Dad?

Susan and Michael Harper, My Family

I've been a dad for some years, and I still don't have any answers. Only big, mind-bending questions like, 'What is that mysterious, semi-buoyant brown crud your children leave in your glass whenever they take a sip of your iced tea?'

Michael Burkett

A couple in Maryland has 'raised' a Cabbage Patch doll as their only son for 19 years. Pat and Joe Posey treat the doll, christened Kevin, as a human. He goes everywhere with them, they talk to him and he 'replies' by Joe putting on his voice. Joe says the doll's favourite hobby is fishing, and father and son go on frequent trips to a pond near their home.

Ananova News website

Don't hold your parents up to contempt. After all, you are their child and it's possible you may take after them.

Evelyn Waugh

Mr Fixit

DIY DADS

My dad, he'd try anything – carpentry, electrical wiring, plumbing, roofing. From watching him, I learned that no matter how difficult a task may seem, if you're not afraid to try it, you can do it. And when you're done, it will leak.

Dave Barry

My dad is Mr Fixit. He cruises the house with a screwdriver in his hand looking for something to tighten.

Rod Lake

- Dad's fixing the dryer.
- Oh dear, you know, ever since the plant cut back his hours, he's spent all his time fixing things. Things that don't need fixing. Things I need, things I use, things I love. I gotta go hide the crock pot.

Eric and Kitty Foreman, That 70s Show

My dad's one of those Mr Fixit guys. Every Sunday morning he'd be locked down in the basement with the power tools. When my sister got married, we had to lead him into the church with a broken toaster.

Mike Rowe

I wish my father wouldn't try to fix things any more, for everything he's mended is more broken than before.

Jack Prelutsky

I tried to get Al to fix the driveway a long time ago. But his philosophy is, why improve a home you're only going to live in anyway?

Peggy Bundy, Married … With Children

Dad taught me all I know about DIY by making an example of our house. Our house was like one of the great European cathedrals: never finished.

Michael Feldman

'What in the world are you doing down there?' Mom would shout down to the basement. 'Just tinkering,' would come Dad's response. He'd be happily rearranging empty paint cans, sorting rusty bent nails from not-so-rusty bent nails and contemplating exactly where to put up a set of shelves.

Allen Delaney, Bay Weekly

Dad showed me the importance of planning for the future by never throwing away anything that 'might come in handy one day'.

William Dane

You know you've turned into your dad the day you put aside a thin piece of wood specifically to stir paint with.

Peter Kay

Whenever I go to Homebase, I always come back with something I didn't need. Because it was a bargain. But I do like a bit of DIY. I put some shelves up. Did it properly. Nice and straight. Then some idiot goes and puts something on them.

Jack Dee

An extra trip to the DIY store is always needed to complete the job.

Douglas Donahue

You wouldn't seek out my dad for advice on a personal problem, but he'd be the first one you'd call when the dishwasher broke or someone flushed a hairpiece down your toilet.

David Sedaris

Fathers' Wit

I looked up to my dad. He was always on a ladder.

David Chartrand

The only person who could start our lawnmower was my father and he could do this only by wrapping the rope around the starter thing and yanking it for a weekend, requiring more time and energy than if he'd cut the entire lawn with his teeth.

Dave Barry

Daddy, Can We Play Monopoly?

FUN, GAMES AND SPORT

Is there any sound more terrifying on a Sunday afternoon than a child asking, 'Daddy, can we play Monopoly?'

Jeremy Clarkson

– Come on, Toby, your go. Quick, quick. Ah, four. No, I'll do it. One, two, three, four. Hmm, Mayfair. My property. My hotel. That'll be £2,000, please, son. Yes, I know you've only got £300 left but you must learn the value of money. I'll make out an IOU and take it out of your pocket money, charging interest at the current rate.

Simon Johnson, 'Competitive Dad', The Fast Show

As I'm sitting there playing with Barbie, washing her hair, I suddenly think, man, I gotta get a Scotch and get the hell outta all this … Look at me, *I'm bathing dolls!*

Tim Allen

I knew I was an unwanted baby when I saw that my bath toys were a toaster and a radio. My parents gave me a rattle that was still attached to the snake.

Joan Rivers

Daddy, Can We Play Monopoly?

My parents put a live teddy bear in my crib.

Woody Allen

Everyone who ever walked barefoot into his child's room late at night hates Lego.

Tony Kornheiser

I'd say half of all our Lego has been through this kid.

Reese Wilkerson, Malcolm in the Middle

My father used to play with my brother and me in the yard. Mother would come out and say, 'You're tearing up the grass.' 'We're not raising grass,' Dad would reply, 'we're raising boys.'

Harmon Killebrew

Play is the work of children. It's very serious stuff.

Bob Keeshan

The greater the mind, the greater the need for play.

Mr Spock, Star Trek

I took the day off work to take care of my son. First we did finger-painting, then we played Snakes and Ladders, then we read a story, then we watched a video, then we played Snakes and Ladders again, then we sang nursery rhymes, then we played football, and by that time it was nearly nine o'clock – in the morning.

Simon Wilson

One time I had to go out, so I asked Woody Allen to watch the children. When I returned less than an hour later, he was throwing his hats and gloves into the fire. The kids were ecstatic. Woody just shrugged and said, 'I ran out of things to do.'

Mia Farrow

Fathers' Wit

Give a kid enough rope and he will trip you up.

Laurence J. Peter

Children's Books That Didn't Make It: *You Were an Accident*; *Hammers, Screwdrivers and Scissors: An I-Can-Do-It Book*; *Some Kittens Can Fly*; *That's It, I'm Putting You Up for Adoption*; *Strangers Have the Best Candy*; *Things Rich Kids Have, But You Never Will*; *Daddy Drinks Because You Cry*.

Anon

You know my father's favorite game? 'C'mere and pull my finger'.

Bill Cosby

Better to play 15 minutes enjoyably and then say, 'Now I'm going to read my paper,' than to spend all day at the zoo crossly.

Dr Benjamin Spock

My father took me to the zoo. He told me to go over to the leopard and play connect the dots.

Rodney Dangerfield

When I was a kid, I asked my dad if I could go ice-skating. He told me to wait until it gets warmer.

Rodney Dangerfield

I was introduced to movies at an early age. For three days after my birth, my father projected *Gone With the Wind* on the living-room wall.

Asia Argento

There is a God and his name is Nickelodeon. God bless.

Brian Holmes

Daddy, Can We Play Monopoly?

My dad was a joker. Whenever I misbehaved, he would bury me in the backyard. Only up to the waist, but you can get real dizzy when all the blood rushes to your head.

Emo Philips

The secret of fatherhood is know when to stop tickling.

Annie Pigeon

My father was very hairy. When my brother and I were little, he liked to amuse us by setting his chest hairs alight and then blowing them out.

Grace White

Children always know when company is in the living room. They can hear their mother laughing at their father's jokes.

Anon

I don't think I've ever had one visit to the park with my kids that didn't end up with somebody needing stitches in casualty.

Dave Lacey

Come on, son, I challenge you at a video game … Oh, I didn't know you could die in the training room.

Frasier Crane, Frasier

The so-called games of skill at amusement parks are tough on dads. They are often the first chance your kids get to watch you fail extravagantly and in plain sight.

Hugh O'Neill

The child had every toy his father wanted.

Colin Wilks

Fathers' Wit

My father gave me a bat for Christmas. The first time I tried to play with it, it flew away.

Rodney Dangerfield

Pay no attention to the statements on boxes that say things like 'For ages 1–3'. The best toy for a child aged 0–3 is a toy that says 'For ages 10–14'. The best toy for a child aged 10–14 is cash, or its own apartment.

Dave Barry

The best toy you ever have as a kid is a big brown cardboard box to play with. Because, as a kid, this is the closest you're going to come to having your own apartment. You can crawl in, 'I'll live here from now on.' Cut a hole for a window, stick your head out.

Jerry Seinfeld

– I spy with my little eye something beginning with 'u'.
– Unicorn? Unicycle? Uniform? I give up.
– Onions!

Frank Tripp

When I was a baby, my father used to throw me up in the air and then go and answer the phone.

Rita Rudner

I said to my old man, 'How can I get my kite in the air?' He said, 'Run off a cliff.'

Rodney Dangerfield

The worst sensation I know of is getting up at night and stepping on a toy train.

Kin Hubbard

Daddy, Can We Play Monopoly?

A 3-year-old child is a being who gets almost as much fun out of a $56 set of swings as it does out of finding a small green worm.

Bill Vaughan

My son uses his unbreakable toy to break his other toys.

Paul Adams

Daddy's favourite tools are numbered among a child's favourite toys. Every kid wants to get her hands on Dad's retracting tape measure and his hammer.

St Clair Adams Sullivan

When you give a child a hammer, everything becomes a nail.

Leo Kaplan

From the first tentative kicks of a toddler in the backyard to the pub banter of fathers and grown sons, football is a glue that holds many a man and son together through the years.

Tom Beardshaw

My dad gave me only one piece of advice. He said, 'Son, you can do anything you like so long as you never support Everton.'

Des Merton

Frank Lampard is a great football player. He used to be my son. Now I'm his father.

Frank Lampard Sr

A father's solemn duty is to take his children to football matches and teach them what to shout at the ref.

Jasmine Birtles

Fathers' Wit

I took my daughter to her very first Red Sox game three months before she was born. Some folks would argue that I actually took my wife and that my daughter was along *in utero* just for the ride. They would be wrong. My wife had zero interest in going. Just this once I pleaded. I desperately wanted to expose my unborn child to the lullaby of Fenway much as some deranged parents lay Mozart on the pregnant woman.

Mark Starr

For the parent of a Little Leaguer, a baseball game is simply a nervous breakdown divided into innings.

Earl Wilson

If you lose, son, you're out of the family.

Homer Simpson

– Alex played baseball today! Tell Mummy what you hit!
– Daddy's head.

Nicky and Alex Katsopolis, Full House

> Baseball may be the nation's game
> With throw and run and hit;
> But first among the skills, it seems,
> Is learning how to spit.

Art Buck

Son, when you participate in sporting events, it's not whether you win or lose, it's how drunk you get.

Homer Simpson

Father's Day

Father's Day is the same as Mother's Day but you don't spend as much.

Bill Cosby

Father's Day is the day when father goes broke giving his family money so they can surprise him with gifts he doesn't need.

Richard Taylor

My kids hate me. Every Father's Day they give a 'World's Greatest Dad' mug to the milkman.

Rodney Dangerfield

We never marked Father's Day when I was a boy and I suspect that my own father would have thrown up if we had.

Tom Kemp

I got my dad one of those typical Father's Day cards, with a picture of a hunting coat hanging on a peg, a decoy duck and some golf clubs leaning in the corner. It's the perfect card for him, because there's nothing Dad loves more than going out in the woods on a frosty morning and beating ducks to death with a four-iron.

Danny Liebert

I hate Father's Day because I can never find the right card. They're all too nice.

Margaret Smith

Things You Don't Want to Hear from Your Kids on Father's Day: They were out of ties so we got you a prairie dog; We all chipped in and got you a less humiliating hairpiece.

David Letterman

I have mixed emotions when I receive my Father's Day gifts. I'm glad my kids remember me. I'm disappointed that they actually think I dress like that.

Mike Dugan

My kids keep saying, 'I don't know what to get you,' but everything they buy, sooner or later your wife has to give away to the Salvation Army, or maybe you find the kids washing the car with it.

Bill Cosby

My husband's not the romantic type. For Mother's Day, he gave me a George Foreman grill. For Father's Day, I gave it him back, in a sort of forceful upward motion.

Sandi Selvi

Last year on Father's Day, my son gave me something I've always wanted: the keys to my car.

Al Sterling

The most memorable Father's Day present I ever got was a pair of slippers – those furry things with rabbit ears and rabbit eyes. I went downstairs and our dog is old and his sight is not good. He thought they were two rabbits attacking me, and he ate them while they were on my feet.

Bill Cosby

Two years ago, my Father's Day present was a hose reel. Last year it was a set of nozzles. See a pattern here? I guess it's

hard to know what to get the man who provided
everything.

Michael Feldman

What Dads Say

How many times do I have to tell you?
I don't care what 'everyone' is doing.
Are you deaf or something?
I don't care who else is going.
Do you think I'm made of money?
Who'll end up feeding it and taking it for a walk?
Money doesn't grow on trees.
After all we do for you.
You don't know how lucky you are.
I hope someday you have kids just like you.
How do you know you don't like it if you haven't tasted it?
Don't speak with your mouth full.
Don't sit so close to the television.
I won't tell you again.
I didn't ask who put it there, I said, 'Pick it up.'
If I've told you once, I've told you a thousand times.
It must be somewhere.
Is that what you're going to wear?
Over my dead body.
Because I say so, that's why.
Someday you'll thank me.
What did I just say?
Stop crying or I'll give you something to cry about.
Wipe your shoes before you come through that door.
Take your feet off the sofa.
You'll have someone's eye out with that.
Don't ever let me catch you doing that again.
B-E-D spells bed.

Fathers' Wit

Don't get smart with me.
When I was a little boy ...
Get a haircut!
You have enough dirt in your ears to grow potatoes.
You take after your mother.
Don't come crying to me.
Do it to make your mother happy.
If the wind changes, you'll stay that way.
You're old enough to know better.
Wait till you have children of your own.
It's such a lovely day. Why don't you go and play in the
garden? Oh, take the rubbish to the bin while you're at it.
As long as you live under my roof, you'll do as I say.
Because I'm your father, that's why.
Close the door! You don't live in a barn.
You'd better ask your mother.

Things you won't hear a father say: 'Go ahead, take my car –
and here's 50 bucks for gas'; 'Here, you take the remote';
'Can you turn up that music? It really calms my nerves';
'Waiter! More ice cream for the little one!'

David Letterman

My dad is a fount of crap jokes and sayings ... If he hears
someone in a restaurant dropping glasses or cutlery, he
shouts, 'Sack the juggler!' If we are out on a drive in
Scotland and he sees a hill, he recites, 'On yonder hill, there
stood a coo; it mood awa', it's not there noo.' And if you're
ever stupid enough to say, 'Excuse me, please' on passing
him in the hallway, he will lock you in a bear hug saying, 'I
thought you said squeeze me, please.'

Pink Strat, b3ta.com

All my dad ever says is, 'Mmm, that'll be nice.' 'Dad, there's a
meteorite heading for England resulting in certain death for
the entire population.' 'Mmm, that'll be nice.' 'Dad, I'm

about to stab you with this big sharp thing.' 'Mmm, that'll be nice.'

Gary, Men Behaving Badly

After a meal my dad always says, 'Good thing we ate when we did because I'm not a bit hungry now.'

Pukearrhea, b3ta.com

I've been accident-prone most of my life and have ended up in A&E more than a few times. No matter what has happened to me, my dad's favourite thing is always to ask, 'Doctor, will she still be able to play the piano?' When the doctor affirms that yes, I'll still be able to play the piano, he always responds with the same, 'Funny, she couldn't before … '

Pink Strat, b3ta.com

My arse!

Jim Royle, The Royle Family

I Want it Now!

SPOILT BRATS

- I want it *now*, Daddy!
- Veruca, sweetheart, I'm not a magician.
- You're a rotten, mean father. You never give me anything I want.

Veruca and Henry Salt, Willy Wonka and the Chocolate Factory

For the last nine million years, children have had just one guiding philosophy and it is greed: *Mine! Mine! Mine!*

Bill Cosby

Fathers' Wit

I'll thcream and thcream and thcream till I'm thick.

Violet Elizabeth, Just William

– You're bribing your daughter with a car?
– Ah, c'mon, isn't 'bribe' just another word for 'love'?

Lois and Peter Griffin, Family Guy

The daughter who is her father's indulged 'little princess' may spend the rest of her life stamping her foot when she doesn't get her way, or pulling away when a love affair hits rough water, or becoming a fair-weather friend.

Victoria Secunda

– Earl, you'll spoil him.
– I just want him to like me. Is that so wrong?

Fran and Earl Sinclair, Dinosaur

A truly appreciative child will break, lose, spoil, or fondle to death any really successful gift within a matter of minutes.

Russell Lynes

The excessive regard of parents for their children, and their dislike of other people's, is, like class feeling, patriotism, save-your-soul-ism and other virtues, a mean exclusiveness at bottom.

Thomas Hardy

If the children's name for me is Dad-Can-I, then my name for them is Yes-You-May.

Bill Cosby

The problem is I like him too much and he knows it.

Bobby Knight

I Want it Now!

The thing that impresses me most about America is the way the parents obey their children.

Duke of Windsor

Americans do not rear children, they *incite* them: they give them food and shelter and applause.

Randall Jarrell

How can one say no to a child? How can one be anything but a slave to one's own flesh and blood?

Henry Miller

If you want to see what children can do, you must stop giving them things.

Norman Douglas

I have never seen a happy spoilt child or adult.

Tom Lacey

Whenever I mentioned to my father that I wanted a television set, his stock reply was, 'People in Hell want ice water.'

Garrison Keillor

I'd like to thank my parents for giving me the gift of poverty.

Roberto Begnini, in his Oscar acceptance speech

A child, like your stomach, doesn't need all that you can afford to give it.

Franklin A. Clark

Your children need your presence more than your presents.

Jesse Jackson

Fathers' Wit

My father was always carrying me in his arms, giving me loud, moist kisses and calling me pet names like 'little sparrow' and 'little fly'. Once I ruined a tablecloth with a pair of scissors. My mother spanked me across the hand until it hurt. I cried so hard that my father came and took me by the hand. He kissed me and comforted me and quieted me down.

Svetlana Aliluyeva on her father, Joseph Stalin

When a father is indulgent, he is more indulgent than a mother. Little ones treat their mother as the authority of rule, and their father as the authority of dispensation.

Frederick Faber

A lot of today's new parents are annoying, giving their kids time-outs for slaying their friends, strapping safety helmets on them every time they walk down a flight of stairs, and displaying those stupid 'Baby on Board' stickers in their cars. They just wanna protect their kids at every moment from every thing. Have they considered large safe-deposit boxes with air holes?

Bill Geist

Hell, our kids used to stand up in the passenger seat while we drove. (On our way to the grocery store to buy sugar-coated lead paint flakes for breakfast.)

Bill Geist

My father said there are four things a child needs: plenty of love, nourishing food, regular sleep, and lots of soap and water. After that, what he needs most is some intelligent neglect.

Ivy Baker Priest

Perhaps a child who is fussed over gets a feeling of destiny, he thinks he is in the world for something important and it gives him drive and confidence.

Dr Benjamin Spock

Never fear spoiling children by making them too happy.
Happiness is the atmosphere in which all good affections
grow.

Thomas Bray

Wait 'til Your Father Gets Home

DISCIPLINE

Children today are tyrants. They have no respect for their
elders, flout authority and have appalling manners. What
terrible creatures will they grow up into?

Socrates

My wife and I have many things in common the greatest of
which is that we are both afraid of the children.

Bill Cosby

The modern child will answer you back before you've said
anything.

Laurence J. Peter

> Speak roughly to your little boy,
> And beat him when he sneezes;
> He only does it to annoy,
> Because he knows it teases.

Lewis Carroll

– If you two brats don't get to bed, I'll break your necks!
– Olly, you should treat them with kindness. As the adage
goes, 'You can lead a horse to water, but a pencil must be
lead.'

Oliver Hardy and Stan Laurel, Brats

Fathers' Wit

Cosby's First Law of Intergenerational Perversity: no matter what you tell your child to do, he will always do the opposite.

Bill Cosby

One of the first things one notices in a backward country is that children are still obeying their parents.

Anon

I am not the boss of my house. I don't know how I lost it. I don't know where I lost it. I don't think I ever had it. But I've seen the boss's job … and I don't want it.

Bill Cosby

Things a father should know: how to say 'That's final' and not go back on it as soon as his wife's out of sight.

Katharine Whitehorn

Children have a sixth sense. They can smell the chemistry of parental resolve in the air.

Steve Martini

– Dad, you're a tyrannical fascist.
– Did you just call me a dinosaur?

Randy and Tim Taylor, Home Improvement

Don't go into Mr McGregor's garden: your father had an accident there; he was put in a pie by Mrs McGregor.

Beatrix Potter, The Tale of Peter Rabbit

I'm ashamed to be your father. You're a disgrace to the family name of Wagstaff, if such a thing is possible.

Groucho Marx

Wait 'til Your Father Gets Home

Children with Hyacinth's temperament don't know better as they grow older; they merely know more.

Saki

I can do one of two things: I can be President of the United States or I can control Alice. I cannot possibly do both.

Theodore Roosevelt

> There was a little girl
> Who had a little curl
> Right in the middle of her forehead.
> When she was good
> She was very very good
> And when she was bad
> She was horrid.

Mother Goose

Children of Progressive Parents Admitted Only on Leads.

Notice in London restaurant

Patience and restraint is what parents have when there are witnesses.

Franklin P. Jones

'He's tired'; 'She's teething'; 'He's a real boy'; 'She's a bit of a tomboy' are all euphemisms for 'Whatabrat!'

Tom Kaplan

Yeah, kid, you won't be smiling when we send you a postcard from Disneyland!

Raymond Barone, Everybody Loves Raymond

My father was frightened of his father. I was frightened of my father, and I am damned well going to see to it that my children are frightened of me.

King George V

Fathers' Wit

The Victorians had too much sense to converse with children as though they were human beings.

Clarence Day

One time, I was mad at my parents and I said to them, 'I hate both of you! I'm running away from home!' And my father lifted me up over his head, and said, 'How far do you want to go?' He didn't know I was THE BILL COSBY.

Bill Cosby

All fathers are intimidating. They're intimidating because they are fathers. Once a man has children, for the rest of his life, his attitude is, 'To hell with the world, I can make my own people. I'll eat whenever I want, I'll wear whatever I want, and I'll create whoever I want.'

Jerry Seinfeld

A father's words are like a thermostat that sets the temperature in the house.

Paul Lewis

My father wore the trousers in the family – at least, after the court order.

Vernon Chapman

We all knew Dad was the one in charge: he had control of the remote.

Raymond Bell

In dealing with my children I always keep one thing in mind: we're bigger than they are, and it's our house.

Moss Hart

Wait 'til Your Father Gets Home

If you've never seen a real, fully developed look of disgust, tell your son how you conducted yourself when you were a boy.

Kin Hubbard

After a sleepover, my daughter is returned by her friend's mother who tells me what a lovely child we're raising – so polite, so helpful – I want that child!

Jason Rose

When the kids have their friends round, I have to pretend to be 'Fun Dad' so they won't go back to their parents and say, 'He was really shouty.'

Jonathan Ross

Like any father, I have moments when I wonder whether I belong to the children or they belong to me.

Bob Hope

Who's the father in this house, anyway? Fucking $3 million house and my kids make me stand outside to smoke.

Ozzy Osbourne

It's not a bad thing that children should occasionally, and politely, put parents in their place.

Colette

'I don't want to hear any more about it,' is what you say to your child after you have just lost the argument.

Rod Lake

– Dad, you haven't heard anything I've said!
– You've not been standing in front of 30 million decibels for 35 years. Write me a fucking note!

Kelly and Ozzy Osbourne

– Dad, you never listen. Do you just hear what you want to hear?

– Oh, why, thank you, son. I *have* been working out.

Matt and Victor Pellet, In-Laws

Hey, just because I don't care doesn't mean I'm not listening.

Homer Simpson

When they put parents on a CD maybe then I'll listen.

Bart Simpson

Don't worry that your kids never listen to you. Worry that they are always watching you.

Robert Fulghum

Children have never been very good at listening to their elders, but they have never failed to imitate them.

James Baldwin

The words a father speaks to his children in the privacy of the home are not overheard at the time, but, as in whispering galleries, they will be clearly heard at the end and by posterity.

Jean Paul Richter

If you want your children to improve, let them overhear the nice things you say about them to others.

Haim Ginott

To bring up a child in the way he should go, travel that way yourself once in a while.

Josh Billings

Wait 'til Your Father Gets Home

Setting an example to your children takes all the fun out of middle age.

William Feather

O-oh, Junior's learned to say my 'Ouch-I-hit-my-thumb-with-the-hammer' word.

David Letterman

Diogenes struck the father when the son swore.

Robert Burton

In spite of the 7,000 books of expert advice, the right way to discipline a child is still a mystery to most fathers. Only your grandmother and Genghis Khan know how to do it.

Bill Cosby

I know from experience that I myself benefited from being whipped as a child so I want and command you to whip my son when he is bad and to make him understand why.

Henry IV, to his son's tutor

Children are never too tender to be whipped. Like tough beefsteaks, the more you beat them, the more tender they become.

Edgar Allan Poe

My father only hit me once. But he used a Volvo.

Bob Monkhouse

I didn't know that fathers are not supposed to hit kids if they were bad. Most fathers hit kids – anybody's. The kid whose father didn't hit felt that his father either wasn't interested in him or wasn't his real father.

Sam Levinson

Beat your child every day. You may not know why, but they will.

Joey Adams

If you strike a child, take care that you strike it in anger, even at the risk of maiming it for life. A blow in cold blood neither can nor should be forgiven.

George Bernard Shaw

My father never raised his hand to any one of his children – except in self-defence.

Fred Allen

When Dad got mad he never actually hit me. He'd wiggle his waistband and say, 'Do I have to go for the belt?'

Jay Leno

There's not a man in America who at one time or another hasn't had a secret desire to boot a child in the ass.

W. C. Fields

I remember when it used to be fashionable to spank your kid. My dad would say to me, 'This hurts me worse than it does you.' I wanted to say, 'You bend over then.'

Liz Sells

Spanking takes less time than reasoning and penetrates sooner to the seat of memory.

Will Durant

Wait 'til Your Father Gets Home

I was spanked a few times, and all it did to me was now I like to get spanked.

Sarah Silverman

I don't spank my kids. I find waving the gun around gets the same job done.

Denis Leary

Never beat your children – the world will beat them enough.

Anon

Why do parents always take their children to supermarkets to smack them?

Anon

People who are pro-smacking children say things like, 'It's the only language they understand.' You could apply that to tourists.

Jack Dee

Never raise your hand to your children. It leaves your midsection unprotected.

Red Buttons

My father used to ground me – and then run electricity through me.

Taylor Negron

The best time to tackle a minor problem is before he grows up.

Ray Freedman

Fathers' Wit

In my Rogues' Gallery of repulsive small boys I suppose he would come about third.

P. G. Wodehouse

There's no such thing as a tough child. If you parboil them first for seven hours, they always come out tender.

W. C. Fields

When I have a kid, I want to buy a twin-stroller and put him in one side and then say, 'You had a brother but he was very bad …'

Steven Wright

Even very young children need to be informed about dying. Explain the concept of death very carefully to your child. This will make threatening him with it much more effective.

P. J. O'Rourke

I want you to stop doing that. I'll count to three: 1 … 2 … 2½ … 2¾ … I don't know any more fractions …

Raymond Barone, Everybody Loves Raymond

The rule is, never give a child a choice.

Robert Frost

– Will you brats stop squabbling and play quietly.
– Yes, if you must make a noise make it quietly.

Oliver Hardy and Stan Laurel, Brats

Quiet, kids! If I hear one more word, Bart doesn't get to watch cartoons, and Lisa doesn't go to college.

Homer Simpson

Wait 'til Your Father Gets Home

Hushabye babies
(Hush quite a lot)
Bad babies get rabies
(And have to be shot).

W. C. Sellar and R. J. Yeatman

I was much distressed by the next-door people who had twin babies and played the violin: but one of the twins died, and the other has eaten the fiddle – so all is peace.

Edward Lear

The servant has come for the little Browns this morning – they have been a toothache to me which I shall enjoy the riddance of. Their little voices are like wasps' stings.

John Keats

What is more enchanting than the voices of young people when you can't hear what they say?

Logan Pearsall Smith

Children should be seen and not heard.

Aristophanes

You can't punish me. I'm Angelica! Your princess! Your cupcake! Your little tax shelter!

Angelica, Rugrats

'Go to your room' used to be a punishment. Now when a child is sent to their room it's full of so many luxuries – TV, computers, games and toys – that there's no sense of deprivation.

Brian Connors

Father never punished us. A look was enough, and more than enough.

Mark Twain

Fathers' Wit

One of the gravest rebukes which I can remember to have received from my father was for my disrespect, when I was 12 years old, in taking from the bookshelves a thick old Bible in order to enable me to sit more conveniently at my dinner.

Coventry Patmore

'I brought you into this world,' my father would say, 'and I can take you out. It don't make no difference to me. I'll make another one just like you.'

Bill Cosby

If anything happens to Matt before I get the chance to kill him, I'll never forgive myself.

Victor Pellet, In-Laws

Re: raising kids: Love, without discipline, isn't.

Malcolm Forbes

One parent is enough to spoil you but discipline takes two.

Clive James

My parental tactics run the gamut from moving speeches on racial pride to outright bribery in the form of cold cash.

Bill Cosby

Look, kid, I'm begging you, if you promise not to tell your mother what I did, I'll let you squash something.

Mitch Hogan

If there is anything that we wish to change in the child, we should first examine it and see whether it is not something that could be better changed in ourselves.

Carl Jung

Wait 'til Your Father Gets Home

Always obey your parents, when they are present.

Mark Twain

Because of their size, parents may be difficult to discipline properly.

P. J. O'Rourke

Every time my dad and I got into an argument, we made up over a nice cold beer. I think that's one of the reasons I was taken into care when I was 7.

Lee Harvey

My father is in a bad mood. That means he is feeling better.

Sue Townsend, The Secret Diary of Adrian Mole Aged 13¾

My father is the most even-tempered man in the Navy: he is always in a rage.

Elizabeth King

My father was often angry when I was most like him.

Lillian Hellman

No one used revenge better than my father. I always imagined that scene in *The Godfather*, where some guy wakes up with a horse head next to him, was probably my dad's idea of a get-well greeting card.

Ruby Wax

The secret of dealing successfully with a child is not to be its parent.

Mell Lazarus

I remember the time I was kidnapped and they sent a piece of my finger to my father. He asked for more proof.

Rodney Dangerfield

Fathers' Wit

My parents finally realize that I'm kidnapped and they snap into action immediately: they rent out my room.

Woody Allen

Daddy, I don't want to be an orphan. I saw *Annie*. Orphans have to eat gruel and tap dance with mops.

Emily Tait

– All right, Ally, you have to do what Mommy says.
– Why?
– Because I do.

Raymond and Ally Barone, Everybody Loves Raymond

Let the child's first lesson be obedience, and the second will be what thou wilt.

Benjamin Franklin

Physically there is nothing to distinguish human society from the farmyard except that children are more troublesome and costly than chickens.

George Bernard Shaw

Oh, we've just gotta have that kid over here more often. He makes our kids seem less odd.

Dan Conner, Roseanne

In moments of deepest despair, look at other people's children and console yourself with the thought that yours aren't that bad. (If they *are* that bad, go to the juvenile court and seek consolation there. If you're still in despair, you're probably right.)

Gyles Brandreth

The irritating thing about badly behaved children is that they so often make as orderly and valuable men and women as the other kind.

Mark Twain

Wait 'til Your Father Gets Home

My father's technique was much harder than it looked, like most works of art. If a kid was rude to him, he was usually rude right back: 'I wouldn't take it from a grown-up; why should I take it from you?'

Wilfred Sheed

My father let me walk behind him with a loaded gun, at 7 use an axe, drive his Ford car at 12. My freedom was complete, all he asked for was responsibility in turn.

Charles A. Lindbergh Jr

During the Blitz I was asked if I wanted to have my books or my son evacuated to the safety of the country. I chose my books because many of them were irreplaceable but I could always have another son.

Evelyn Waugh

Little known fact: if you yell for eight years, seven months and six days continuously, you will have produced only enough sound energy to heat one cup of coffee.

James Rawson

Parents are not really interested in justice. They just want peace.

Bill Cosby

Universal peace sounds ridiculous to the head of the average family.

Kin Hubbard

Children are immune to stress but are carriers.

John Spender

Never underestimate a child's ability to get into more trouble.

Martin Mull

Fathers' Wit

Children need to get into trouble to learn how to get out of trouble.

Steven Drayton

The energy which makes a child hard to manage is the energy which afterward makes him a manager of life.

Henry Ward Beecher

When I did something really bad – like lying – my father put me to bed and threatened to make me go without dinner. He never once carried out the threat about no dinner. After a while, he'd open the bedroom door and say, 'Put your clothes on and come down to dinner. I don't know why I should have to eat that dinner and not you.'

Arthur Marx, son of Groucho

How easily a father's tenderness is recalled, and how quickly a son's offences vanish, at the slightest word of repentance.

Molière

Encouragement after censure is as the sun after a shower.

Johann Wolfgang von Goethe

One motivation is worth ten threats, two pressures and six reminders.

Paul Sweeney

Remember that children, marriages and flower gardens reflect the kind of care they get.

H. Jackson Brown Jr

In parenthood (as in business, politics and war) the correlation between the efforts of the people in charge

and the results – dazzling or disastrous – appears
negligible.

Nigel Foulkes

You may be a pain in the ass, you may be bad, but child, you
belong to me.

Ray Charles

Feeding the Mouth That Bites You

FOOD AND DRINK

– Okay, kid, let's order some food.
– Thirty packs of ketchup.

Sonny Koufax and Julian, Big Daddy

There are times when parenthood seems nothing but
feeding the mouth that bites you.

Peter de Vries

The book says to feed the baby every two hours, but do
you count from when you start, or when you finish? It
takes me two hours to get her to eat, and by the time
she's done, it's time to start again, so that I'm feeding her
all the time.

Peter Mitchell, Three Men and a Baby

Some of those Gerber baby desserts are actually pretty
good. Gerber Apple and Blackberry Crumble Dessert tastes
so good I served it at a dinner party.

Pete Austen

Fathers' Wit

When Gerber started selling baby food in Africa, they used the same packaging as in the United States, with the beautiful baby on the label. They withdrew the product and redesigned the label when it was discovered that in Africa companies routinely put pictures of what's inside on the label of products, since many people are illiterate.

Anon

What's the difference between sprouts and bogies? You can't get kids to eat sprouts.

Anon

Carrots? I don't know what company makes this stuff, but I hate it.

Dewey Wilkerson, Malcolm in the Middle

Son, if you don't eat your peas, your widget won't grow.

Gordon Ramsay, Hell's Kitchen Revisited

– Dad, no one could eat this crud.
– Hey, if you don't finish your crud, you're not gonna get any crap for dessert.

Becky and Dan Conner, Roseanne

– Dad, there's a message in my cereal. It says, 'Ooooooo.'
– Peter, those are Cheerios.

Peter and Brian Griffin, Family Guy

I loved giving breakfast to the girls, and I loved it after Abigail became old enough to understand that, remarkable as I was, I did not deserve total credit for making such good corn flakes.

Calvin Trillin

Obtain a large plastic milk jug. Fill halfway with water. Suspend from the ceiling with a cord. Start the jug swinging. Try to insert spoonfuls of soggy cereal such as Fruit Loops or Cheerios into the mouth of the jug while pretending to be an airplane. Now dump the contents of the jug on the floor. Congratulations, you have passed the baby-feeding test.

Anon

I've tried feeding him his broccoli airplane-style but it's no good. Damn him. Damn the broccoli. And damn the Wright Brothers.

Peter Griffin, Family Guy

When I was a kid, my dad used to say to me, 'Eat your peas. It'll put hair on your chest.' I'm five. I'm Italian. I already have hair on my chest.

Maria Menozzi

My kid won't eat cereal unless it turns the milk purple.

Anon

To try and get my kid to eat I'd sometimes say, 'Just pretend it's sand.'

Michael Todd

Kids love to play the dropping game at mealtimes, but you can beat that. You have only to fasten a rubber band on the cup handle and wrap it around the child's wrist. That way the kid digs the rubber band and has all the fun of dropping the cup too.

Bill Cosby

Son, go easy on the orange juice. That stuff doesn't grow on trees – wait, it does. So why is it so damned expensive?

Hal Wilkerson, Malcolm in the Middle

Fathers' Wit

Little kids in supermarkets buy cereal the way men buy lingerie. They get stuff they have no interest in just to get the prize inside.

Jeff Foxworthy

I tell kids they should throw away the cereal and eat the box. At least they'd get some fibre.

Dr Richard Holstein

This would be a better world for children if parents had to eat the spinach.

Groucho Marx

My dad's so impatient. He stands in front of the microwave going, 'Come on! It's been ten seconds. I don't have all minute!'

Cathy Ladman

Never ask a three-year-old to hold a tomato.

Anon

Like food eaten standing up, the food left over on your child's plate contains no calories.

Keith Mayer

Dining out with kids is brilliant. They're the cheapest dates you'll find. They never order the lobster.

David Letterman

How come when a kid looks at an ice cream menu, like a guided missile, they head straight for the most expensive?

Tom Roberts

Low fat? Forget it. When we barbecued, my dad used to take the hamburgers right off the grill, 95 per cent fat, the other 5 per cent lighter fluid.

Jack Coen

Wait 'til Your Father Gets Home

Barbecue: smoke without fire.

Colin Bowles

Men like to barbecue. Men like to cook only if danger is involved.

Rita Rudner

Nothing is more revolting than the spectacle of a normally reasonable father gowned in one of those hot, massive aprons, inscribed with disgustingly corny legends, presiding over a noisome brazier as he destroys huge chunks of good meat and fills the neighbourhood with greasy, acrid smoke: a Boy Scout with five o'clock shadow.

Donald Rogers

A barbecue is a suburban summer ritual at which the eldest male of the household presides over a burnt offering that's undercooked on the inside.

Rick Bayan

A family barbecue? Oh, Al, honey, it's not like we don't enjoy sweltering in the backyard, being bitten by horseflies and watching you scratch your sweaty back with our salad forks but, for once, we'd like to do something *we* want.

Peggy Bundy, Married … With Children

Things you don't want to hear at your family barbecue: 'If you don't wash your hands, it gives the burgers more flavour'; 'Which do you want first, kids? Ice cream or the name of your real father?'

David Letterman

When Dad helped make a chocolate cake the kitchen ended up looking like Willy Wonka had been murdered in there.

Robin Elms

Fathers' Wit

What's for dinner when Mom's away and Dad's 'cooking'?
Well, there's pizza; chips and salsa; Cocoa Puff surprise; cold
pizza; 'Kids Eat Free' night at the local steak house; back-of-
the-fridge goulash (with lots of pepper); but best of all …
whatever's cooking at Grandma's.

David Letterman

I didn't have a great childhood. When I was 7, I said, 'Mom,
what's for dinner?' She said, 'Oh, you're just like your
father.'

Joan Rivers

My dad skinned and cooked my pet rabbit, Blackie, for
dinner. We weren't that hard up. He just fancied a bit of
rabbit.

Johnny Vegas

International Rock Star … Gravy Maker Extraordinaire.

Ozzy Osbourne

The other day I ate at a real nice family restaurant. Every
table had an argument going.

George Carlin

Our son has announced he can't eat meat. What if he starts
wanting to save dolphins and says he has to throw out all
our tuna? I'm only saying this once: I love my kids, but I
will never, never give up my tuna.

Tim Taylor, Home Improvement

In order to know whether a human being is young or old,
offer it food of different kinds at short intervals. If young, it
will eat anything at any hour of the day or night.

Oliver Wendell Holmes

– And you know I don't allow eating in bed.
– I bet you don't say that to Dad.

Susan and Nick Harper, My Family

Do You Think I'm Made of Money?

MONEY MATTERS

Money isn't everything – but it sure keeps you in touch with your children.

John Paul Getty

You need a lot of money to raise a modern child. Hair gel alone will run you thousands of dollars.

Dave Barry

Having kids is so expensive. By the time they're 18 it's cost a quarter of a million pounds. And that's not counting school fees and bail.

Pete Gifford, Cold Feet

It sometimes happens, even in the best families, that a baby is born. This is not necessarily cause for alarm. The important thing is to keep your wits about you and borrow some money.

Anon

I've spent a fortune on my kids' education, and a fortune on their teeth. The difference is, they use their teeth.

Robert Orben

Fathers' Wit

My dad always maintained he didn't care about money.
That's because he never had any.

Louie Anderson

I sometimes wish my father realized he was poor instead of
being that most nerve-racking of phenomena, a rich man
without money.

Peter Ustinov

Bill Gates's baby looks at the baby on the Pampers packet
and thinks: 'I can buy and sell you.'

David Letterman

Mother Nature, in all her infinite wisdom, has instilled
within each of us a powerful biological instinct to
reproduce. This is her way of assuring that the human race,
come what may, will never have any disposable income.

Dave Barry

A married man with a family will do anything for money.

Charles de Talleyrand

When the household expenses shot up very high, Father
would yell his head off. He always did some yelling anyhow,
merely on general principles.

Clarence Day

I was born in very sorry circumstances. My mother was
sorry and my father was sorry as well.

Norman Wisdom

My family was so poor they couldn't afford any kids. The
lady next door had me.

Lee Trevino

Do You Think I'm Made of Money?

We were so poor we had no hot water. But it didn't matter because we had no bathtub to put it in anyway.

Tom Dreesen

Our family was so poor we used to go to Kentucky Fried Chicken and lick other people's fingers.

Lenny Banks

New Year was the only thing we could afford that was really new.

George Burns

I would say we moved around quite a bit. Every time the rent came due, my father carried the furniture on his back to some new place. For 30 years, I thought we were in the furniture business.

Jackie Mason

Saving is a fine thing. Especially when your parents have done it for you.

Winston Churchill

It was tough asking thrifty parents for money. You had to beg your father, 'Dad, can I have a dollar?' And he'd say, 'What happened to the dollar I gave you last year?'

Sinbad

My dad would always pay for things with change. It's one thing to buy the newspaper or candy with change but a shirt or a lamp? That's not right. We'd be standing in line with him while he counted, '$34.50 cents, $34.55 cents, $34.60 cents, $34.65 cents. There you go.'

Ellen DeGeneres

Fathers' Wit

My father was so cheap. When he got engaged to my mother, he didn't buy her a diamond ring. He gave her a lump of coal and told her to be patient.

Cathy Ladman

My dad was so cheap. When I was a kid and the ice cream van came round, he'd say, 'When they play the music, that means they've run out of ice cream.'

Bob Hayden

My dad's spending habits used to drive my mother up the wall. One moment he'd be buying her a diamond ring, the next he'd be bawling her out for not turning off the lights when she left the room.

Arthur Marx, son of Groucho

– But Dad, *why* can't I have it? Our family is rich.
– Your mother and I are rich. You have nothing.

Vanessa and Cliff Huxtable, The Cosby Show

Rich kids and poor kids are alike: both go round huge estates with guns out of their minds on drugs.

Jeremy Hardy

Teenagers know all about sex; they just think that money comes from God.

Paul Ross

My husband is so cheap. On Christmas Eve he fires one shot and tells the kids Santa committed suicide.

Phyllis Diller

After paying for a wedding, about all a father has left to give away is the bride.

Ned Spieker

Do You Think I'm Made of Money?

I pay 85 dollars for a pair of sneakers for him and he's out in the yard riding his bike over them so they don't look new.

Paul Hennessy, 8 Simple Rules for Dating My Teenage Daughter

My daughter wanted some trainers. I said, 'You're 11. Make some!'

Jeremy Hardy

The only thing children wear out faster than shoes is parents.

John J. Plomp

The easy way to teach children the value of money is to borrow from them.

Anon

Yes, I did take money from the children's piggy banks, but I always left an IOU.

W. C. Fields

If a man smiles in his own house someone is sure to ask him for money.

William Feather

I spend my life saying to my kids, 'Okay, so where's my change?'

George Chambers

– Has anyone noticed anything funny about the rabbit?
– Yes. It's been here two days and hasn't asked me for money.

Nick and Ben Harper, My Family

Fathers' Wit

– Darling, when was the last time we received a letter from
  our son?
– Just a second, I'll look in the chequebook.

Anon

I wrote to my daughter at university yesterday. I sent her a
parental haiku:
    Enclosed is cheque
    You bleed me dry
    Stop it

Ben Harper, My Family

– Daddy's cut off my allowance! I told him I'm going to
  hire a lawyer and I'm going to sue him and take all his
  money and then cut *him* off.
– Wow, what did he say to that?
– He said he wouldn't pay for my lawyer.

Rachel and Jill Green, Friends

It is a wise child that owes its own father.

Carolyn Wells

Daddy told me that when he dies he wants his ashes
scattered in Selfridges so he can be sure Mummy and I will
come visit.

Lana Forbes-Carlton

There are three books my daughter felt were the most
important influences in her life: the Bible, her mother's
cookbook and her father's chequebook.

Joyce Mattingly

If you want to recapture your youth, cut off his allowance.

Al Bernstein

Do You Think I'm Made of Money?

In 1700, Charles Seymour, the sixth Duke of Somerset, ordered his two daughters to stand guard over him while he took his afternoon nap. On waking he found one of them was sitting down, so he docked £20,000 from her inheritance. And in 1700, £20,000 really was £20,000.

Frank Muir

A son could bear complacently the death of his father while the loss of his inheritance might drive him to despair.

Niccolò Machiavelli

I have never been a material girl. My father always told me never to love anything that cannot love you back.

Imelda Marcos

Life was a lot simpler when what we honoured was father and mother rather than all major credit cards.

Robert Orben

My father eschewed luxury. He had a strong sense of enoughness.

Calvin Trillin

It now costs more to amuse a child than it once cost to educate his father.

Vaughan Monroe

A boy does not put his hand in his pocket until every other means of gaining his end has failed.

J. M. Barrie

My father told me that if humanly possible one should never lend people money, as it almost inevitably made them hate you.

Lord Rothschild

Fathers' Wit

I haven't taught you anything about the value of money. Basically, it's worthless, but it lets you buy a lot of things that you can enjoy.

Ernest Hemingway

No, you can't charge them rent when they're still in grade school.

Annie Pigeon

Never ask for anything that costs more than five pounds when your dad is filling out his tax return.

Simon Robinson, aged 10

I can't imagine what my kids will tell their kids they had to do without.

Alex Blake

Behind the Wheel

THE FAMILY CAR

For Sale: 1993 Toyota Supra twin turbo, £14,250, very rare, every toy, traction, cruise, private number plate, 160 mph, awesome, girlfriend forgot to take pill, gutted.

Advert in Autotrader *magazine*

Children in back seats cause accidents. Accidents in back seat cause children.

Anon

If you care at all what the inside of your car looks like, you might want to think again about becoming a father.

Jason Wilson

Behind the Wheel

When you're a dad, you can't keep your cool car – fancy stereo, power windows and sunroof. Kids turn an ordinary cookie into a sugar hand grenade. You have to take the car into the shop because chocolate chips are clogging the carburettor.

Sinbad

In a Jeep, you can at least pretend to be cool, like the car is loaded up with equipment for that very dangerous geological expedition. But in a minivan, you're fooling no one. Your side compartments are stuffed with diaper wipes, and the interior is all sticky with apple juice. You're not Indiana Jones, you're a dad.

Paul Reiser

I'm one of seven children. My dad bought an MG sports car once. Nice car, but where the bloody hell were we supposed to sit? We had to go to school like the White Helmets Motorcycle Display team, all balanced on each other's shoulders. My dad'd be at the front, 'Low bridge!'

Jeff Green

My kids wanted a DVD fitted in the headrest of the car. I was against this. I don't want my kids to be spoiled. Why should they have stuff I didn't have when I was a kid? But my wife went ahead and fitted the DVD without telling me. To get my own back, I recorded a three-hour film of the back of my head.

Jack Dee

My dad didn't like people as much as he liked his car. He even introduced it to people. 'It's my Bonneville,' he'd say, 'my family's over there.'

Louie Anderson

Fathers' Wit

– You waxed my car, honey! This is the best thing you
  could give me.
– I gave you three boys.
– But none of them came out this clean.

Tim and Jill Taylor, Home Improvement

My dad would spend ages tinkering under the bonnet of
his Capri. Then it would invariably have to be towed to a
garage to have the damage he'd caused repaired.

Robert Greenway

Classic Car Rule: Whenever a beautiful car – usually the
prized possession of an unsympathetic father – is
introduced at the beginning of a film, that car will be
wrecked by the end of it. (See *Risky Business; Ferris
Bueller's Day Off.*)

Hollywood movie cliché

Yeah, I know some people are against drunk driving – like
cops for example. But, you know, sometimes, you've just got
no choice: those kids gotta get to school.

Dave Attell

My baby used to put up a stink any time we put her in the
car seat to take her for a ride. We found that howling like
wolves made her curious enough to stop crying and listen
to the strange sounds we were making.

Genuine advice in a baby manual

I saw this car with a 'Baby on Board' sticker on the back. I
thought, why don't they use a cushion?

Steven Wright

The problem with a 'Baby on Board' sign is that parents
don't take it down when the baby isn't on board. They

should have a sign saying, 'Baby at Auntie Jean's'. That way we'd know where the baby is so we could adjust our driving.

Arthur Smith

Like many fathers, he had a favourite ritual: to put his whole family in the car and drive somewhere. It didn't matter where. What mattered was that he was behind the wheel.

Signe Hammer

My parents had two constant arguments while they were driving, over how fast my father was going or how much gas was left in the tank. My father had a standard defence for either of these. It was always, 'That's because you're looking at it from an angle. If you were over here, you'd see.'

Jerry Seinfeld

It's tough to feel a sense of control when you've got to stop six times during the half-hour ride to Grandma's.

Hugh O'Neill

Okay, first rule of this car. No breaking wind in my car. The only gas that I want to be smelling is unleaded.

Bernie Mac, The Bernie Mac Show

Don't make me stop this car!

Perennial exasperated father's cry

Fathers' Wit

Are We There Yet?

TRAVEL

Are we there yet?

Perennial question child asks on getting in the car

A vacation is when the family goes away for a rest, accompanied by Mother, who sees that the others get it.

Marcelene Cox

Every year my family would pile into the car for our vacation and drive 80 trillion miles just to prove we couldn't get along in any setting.

Janeane Garofalo

A family vacation is one where you arrive with five bags, four kids and seven I-thought-you-packed-its.

Ivern Ball

Can you abandon a child along a public highway for kicking Daddy's seat for 600 miles?

Erma Bombeck

Next to children on a trip, there is nothing more trying than their father. He doesn't go on a trip to enjoy the scenery and relax. He's on a virtual test-run to prove his car's performance in a grinding show of speed and endurance equalled only on the salt flats testing grounds.

Erma Bombeck

Those were awful, those family driving vacations. Dad insisting on covering as many miles as possible in a day; the two of us, tiny hostages in the back seat, clutching our car sickness bags, straining to see something out of the window as the landscape whizzed by. I was 13 before I realized cows aren't blurry.

Niles Crane, Frasier

Never take a cross-country trip with a kid who has just learned to whistle.

Jean Deuel

Wherever we had to be, we were usually late because Dad was always implementing some plan to beat the traffic.

Ray Romano

'Are you lost, Daddy?' I asked tenderly. 'Shut up,' he explained.

Ring Lardner

If you ever want to torture my dad, tie him up and right in front of him, refold a road map incorrectly.

Cathy Ladman

There are two classes of travel – first class and with children.

Robert Benchley

It has long been my belief that in times of great stress, such as a four-day vacation, the thin veneer of family wears off almost at once, and we are revealed in our true personalities.

Shirley Jackson

I don't understand people who go to amusement parks. I spend most of my time trying not to be nauseous. I feel great today. I think I'll go down to Funland and snap my neck on the back of a ride. Honey, let's take the kids. I want to give them a spinal cord injury for Christmas.

Dom Irrera

Fathers' Wit

Disneyland: purgatory, with better parking space.

Anon

Who needs Disney World? My kids get as much of a thrill when we drive the car through the car wash.

Oliver Coe

Babies don't need a vacation but I still see them at the beach. I'll go over to a little baby and say, 'What are you doing here? You've never worked a day in your life.'

Steven Wright

You emerge from travelling with kiddies looking as if you had just moved the piano upstairs, single-handed.

Robert Benchley

Last year my wife Camille and I found a summer camp that would accept our five children … We watched the bus loaded with our kids disappear, then walked back toward the house. We could *hear* the property. We had never heard our property before. We noticed that the birds were coming back. My wife's face began to twitch and tremble. I said, 'Dear, are you having a stroke?' She answered serenely, 'No, I think I'm going to smile.' I asked her why. She said simply, 'Peace of mind.'

Bill Cosby

What's the point of going out? We're just going to end up back home anyway.

Homer Simpson

Growing Up

As our children grow, so must we grow to meet their changing emotional, intellectual, and designer-footwear needs.

Dave Barry

You know your children are growing up when they start asking questions that have answers.

John J. Plomp

She was growing up, and that was the direction I wanted her to take. Who wants a daughter that grows sideways?

Spike Milligan

Children are angels whose wings decrease as their legs increase.

French proverb

Watching children grow up is a great delight. You see in them your own faults and your wife's virtues, and that can be a very stabilizing influence.

Peter Ustinov

I've noticed that one thing about parents is that no matter what stage your child is in, the parents who have older children always tell you the next stage is worse.

Dave Barry

My 11-year-old daughter mopes around the house all day waiting for her breasts to grow.

Bill Cosby

Boys do not grow up gradually. They move forward in spurts like the hands of the clocks in railway stations.

Cyril Connolly

Fathers' Wit

You know your children are growing up when they stop asking where they came from and refuse to tell you where they're going.

P. J. O'Rourke

I can't decide whether growing pains are something kids have – or are.

Jackson Cole

There's a time – all too brief as it too soon becomes apparent to parents – to be little; a time to be in-between; and a time to be old. Let each have its season. Let little be little.

Malcolm Forbes

Mother nature is wonderful. She gives us 12 years to develop a love for our children before turning them into teenagers.

Eugene Bertin

A pre-teen is sort of like having a tornado before a hurricane hits.

W. Bruce Cameron

The Clearasil Years

TEENAGERS

It's extraordinary. One day, you look at your phone bill and realize your child is a teenager.

Milton Berle

Teenagers are resentful festering grudges in PORN STAR T-shirts. They should be shot into space until they reach their mid-20s.

Anon

When a kid turns 13, stick him in a barrel, nail the lid shut, and feed him through the knothole. When he turns 16, plug the hole.

Mark Twain

If Abraham's son had been a teenager, it wouldn't have been a sacrifice.

Scott Spendlove

Teenagers are God's punishment for having sex.

Patrick Murray

– Son, now you're a teenager, you're not going to be yourself for a few years. You're going to be a little wise guy who smarts off to people, and who a lot of people think is a real jerk.
– Chip off the old block, eh, Dad?

Tim and Randy Taylor, Home Improvement

Get Out of My Life, But First Could You Drive Me and Cheryl to the Mall: A Parent's Guide to the New Teenager

Anthony E. Wolf, book title

When We're in Public, Pretend You Don't Know Me: Surviving Your Daughter's Adolescence So That You Don't Look Like an Idiot and She Still Talks to You

Susan Borowitz, book title

8 Simple Rules for Dating My Teenage Daughter and Other Tips for a Beleaguered Father (Not That Any of Them Work)

W. Bruce Cameron, book title

Fathers' Wit

I'm Okay, You're a Brat: Setting the Priorities Straight and Freeing You from the Guilt and Mad Myths of Parenthood

Susan Jeffers, book title

My friends complain that their teenagers sleep all day. Not me. Can you imagine if they were awake all day?

Buzz Nutley

The teenager seems to have replaced the Communist as the appropriate target for public controversy and foreboding.

Edgar Friedenberg

We must never lower the voting age to 14. That's when they think they know everything.

John Goodwin

You know when you're turning into your parents the first time you say to your teenager: 'You treat this house like it's a hotel.'

David Harrison

When your daughter is 12 she is given a splendidly silly article of clothing called a training bra. To train *what*? I never had a training *jockstrap*.

Bill Cosby

I never intended to be the father of two teenage daughters. If I had been asked, I might have chosen to go for something cheaper, like a stable of racehorses, or something easier to raise, like wolverines.

W. Bruce Cameron

Any astronomer can predict with absolute accuracy exactly where every star in the universe will be at 11.30 tonight. He can make no such prediction about his teenage daughter.

James Adams

– Where are you going?
– Out.
– Out's kind of a big place. Wanna narrow that down?
– Side.

Teddie Cochran and Max Ryan, The Geena Davis Show

I thought teenagers were supposed to lock themselves in
their rooms and never talk to their parents. I was kinda
looking forward to that.

George Lopez, The George Lopez Show

I would prefer it if my son were riding along a riverbank
like something out of Enid Blyton but he prefers hanging
around the supermarket car park skateboarding.

Mark Fielding

No need to worry about your teenagers when they're not
at home. A national survey revealed that they all go to the
place – 'out' – and they all do the same thing there –
'nothing'.

Bruce Lansky

Nobody understands anyone aged 18, including those who
are aged 18.

Jim Bishop

Studies show that the world population of teenagers is on
the rise, and I'm convinced that every single one of them
comes over to my house to eat my food.

W. Bruce Cameron

My daughter brought home one of her 'Goth' friends –
black nail polish, black lipstick, black eyeliner, black hair,
Liquid paper-white face. I'm sorry, didn't we use to call
that 'Halloween'?

Jeff Foxworthy

Fathers' Wit

That child was born gloomy. She named her guinea pigs 'Death' and 'Destruction'; she has an imaginary friend with leukaemia.

Carrie, Carrie and Barry

Have you ever found yourself sneaking into your teenage son's bedroom while he's at school to stare at his posters of nubile pop stars?

Clint Ferris

When I was a teenager, I didn't have any posters over the walls because I didn't like to think I lived with my mum and dad. I liked to think I was just staying there.

Harry Enfield

Adolescence is that period in a kid's life when parents become more difficult.

Ryan O'Neal

Adolescence is a time of rapid change. Between the ages of 12 and 17, for example, a parent can age as much as 20 years.

Anon

A boy becomes an adult three years before his parents think he does, and about two years after *he* thinks he does.

Lewis B. Hershey

There's nothing wrong with teenagers that reasoning with them won't aggravate.

Lionel Rees

Someday you're going to have to tell your dad to go to hell.

Warren Buffet

The Clearasil Years

Every generation revolts against its fathers and makes friends with its grandfathers.

Lewis Mumford

But Dad, I've had loads of life-experience. I'm 18 years old. I've been to sleep-away camps. I had a goldfish who died. I even got on the wrong bus once.

Corenna, Boy Meets World

I was quite a good teenager for about two years till I got in with bigger boys. I thought I was a punk. I wasn't. I was 15, I hated doing any work, and I hated my parents because they were middle class and not on the dole.

Harry Enfield

Rules of Being Teenaged: Your parents are a taxi; Hate your parents but be nice to your friends' parents; Always lie, and if lying doesn't work, lie louder.

Kevin the Teenager, Harry Enfield and Chums

Where have you been? Who have you been with? What have you been doing, and why?

Todd Baxter

Oh, it's soooo unfair!

Kevin the Teenager, Harry Enfield and Chums

When I was a teenager, I used to try to make my head explode by holding my breath, thinking that if I blew up my head, my mom and dad would be sorry.

Kurt Cobain

Talking with my teen is like walking through a minefield – at any time you feel a bomb could blow up in my face.

Thomas Anderson

Fathers' Wit

– Dad, can we get on with this? I have someplace to go.
– TV counts as a place?

David and Rob Sinclair, Dinosaur

– Mum, can I get a tattoo?
– No.
– Dad, can I get a tattoo?
– Only if it says, 'Daddy's Little Sunbeam'.

Susan, Janey and Ben Harper, My Family

– Oh, Kelly, I wish you hadn't got your nose pierced.
  Piercing can become addictive you know. Next thing
  you'll be telling me you want to get a tattoo.
– Dad, I already have a tattoo.

Ozzy and Kelly Osbourne

My father said, 'Never get a tattoo because if you turn to a
life of crime you're easily identifiable.'

Amy Lamé

When I told my dad I wanted a nose ring, he said, 'Have
you considered lightning?'

Bob Hayden

If your kid wants to get a tattoo or a piercing just say, 'Great
idea! As a matter of fact, let's *both* go get tattoos and nose
rings!'

David Letterman

To an adolescent, there is nothing in the world more
embarrassing than a parent.

Dave Barry

The Clearasil Years

– Dad, *please* don't show me up by telling those old stories.
– 'course not … I always remember the day you got
through three pairs of trousers …

Gary and Gary's Dad, Men Behaving Badly

I am the father of teenage girls, which means I have only
one job: to embarrass my daughters.

John Sidley

I know one way guaranteed to make my children scatter
instantly: I get up and dance.

Terry Wogan

My dad still has this knack of embarrassing me. I have this
dream that I'm at Buckingham Palace collecting my MBE
from the Queen for being a smashing guy and he says, 'Do
you know he didn't have a proper girlfriend till he was 19?'

Gary, Men Behaving Badly

As a psychiatrist, I can take comfort in the fact that without
embarrassing parents, there'd be no psychology.

Frasier Crane, Frasier

Psychiatry enables us to correct our faults by confessing our
parents' shortcomings.

Laurence J. Peter

If you really want to embarrass your kid at her school
musical recital evening, pep up the crowd by starting a
Mexican wave.

David Letterman

If your teenager doesn't think you're a real embarrassment
and a hard-nosed bore, you're probably not doing your
job.

Anon

Fathers' Wit

Dad, I want a car. I have the perfect hair for a convertible.

Bridget Hennessy, 8 Simple Rules for Dating
My Teenage Daughter

– Dad, all my friends say that I should have my own car.
– Wonderful. When are they going to buy it?

Denise and Cliff Huxtable, The Cosby Show

A pedestrian is a man who has two cars – one being driven
by his wife, the other by one of his children.

Robert Bradbury

A father and his car keys are soon parted.

Pip Smart

When I was a teenager, every Saturday night I'd ask my
dad for the car keys and he'd always say the same thing:
'All right, son, but don't lose them, because some day we
may get a car.'

Yakov Smirnoff

– It's our son's first trip out in the car since he passed his
test. Haven't you any advice for him?
– No mooning when the car's in gear.

Jill and Tim Taylor, Home Improvement

Signs You May Be Living with a Teenager: Your car
insurance suddenly costs more than your car; Your gas tank
is always empty and your laundry basket is always full.

W. Bruce Cameron

An optimist is a father who lets his teenager borrow the
car. A pessimist is one who won't. A pedestrian is one
who did.

Bob Monkhouse

The Clearasil Years

You'd be amazed how many teenagers get their first car by asking for a motorcycle.

James Varley

Why not give your son a motorcycle for his last birthday?

Colin Bowles

The worst eternal triangle known is teenager, parent and telephone.

Lavonne Mathison

Many a man wishes he were strong enough to tear a telephone book in half – especially if he has a teenage daughter.

Guy Lombardo

The only thing I ever said to my parents when I was a teenager was, 'Hang up, I got it!'

Carol Leifer

The cell phone was invented purely for daughters to call their fathers at any time and you will go get her.

Brad Houston

Called telephone company and announced, 'I want to report an obscene phone bill.'

Edward Grayson

Boys will be boys. And even that wouldn't matter if only we could prevent girls from being girls.

Anthony Hope

The other night, my little teenage daughter came home and said – and I don't think she was being very original – 'Daddy, as an outsider, how do you feel about the human race?'

Lyndon B. Johnson

Fathers' Wit

– Dad, have I ever lied to you?
– Numerous times.
– I meant today.

Tim and Randy Taylor, Home Improvement

Adolescence is when children start trying to bring up their parents.

Richard Armour

Age 17 is the point in the journey when the parents retire to the observation car, when you stop being critical of your eldest son and he starts being critical of you.

James B. Reston

Dad, it's 1.30 a.m., you're drunk and you're wearing an earring. How am I supposed to push against my boundaries if I don't have any? Where's the challenge? It's like I'm Steve McQueen in *The Great Escape* except the Germans have let me out, given me a motorbike and an *A-Z* of Hamburg.

Michael Harper, My Family

Oh, come on, Dad, do you really think what I did was that bad? You grew up in the sixties. I've seen the photo album. Those clothes had to have some pharmaceutical explanation.

Darlene Conner, Roseanne

– This pamphlet lists all the signs your kid may be high. So far, our son has nine out of ten – bloodshot eyes, mood swings, irregular appetite, odd sleeping patterns. Oh, Red, our son *is* high!
– Nonsense. He's not on drugs. He's just weird.

Kitty and Red Foreman, That 70s Show

The Clearasil Years

My father told me marijuana would cause me brain damage – because if he caught me doing it he was going to break my head.

Tom Dreesen

I don't have to talk to my kids about taking drugs because they've seen vans, ambulances, police cars – you name it, at the house, and I've been in a whole bunch of rehabs so I think my behaviour put them off the idea.

Ozzy Osbourne

– I don't want to kick our own daughter and her boyfriend out of the house for good. I just hate to see them struggle.
– Fair enough. We won't visit them.

Roseanne and Dan Conner, Roseanne

Few things are more satisfying than seeing your children have teenagers of their own.

Doug Larson

– Turn that racket down! It sounds like they're banging their heads on their guitars while they're getting their teeth drilled.
– Hey, cool, Dad – you saw the video.

Tim and Randy Taylor, Home Improvement

You know what would end Madonna's career? If enough parents suddenly started to like her.

Bill Cosby

If I'm more of an influence on your son as a rapper than you are as a father, you've got to look at yourself as a parent.

Ice Cube

When I was a boy of 14, my father was so ignorant I could hardly stand to have the old man around. But when I got to be 21, I was astonished at how much he had learned in seven years.

Mark Twain

We Don't Need No Education

– Dad, why do I have to go to school?
– School is a place you go to be out of this house.

Ray and Tony Flynn, The Tony Flynn Show

To my father a school was not a seat of learning but a noisy detention compound to which children were sent for long periods of the year in order to be removed from under their parents' feet.

R. F. Delderfield

School is where you go between when your parents can't take you and industry can't take you.

John Updike

My very first day of school, my parents dropped me off at the wrong nursery. I didn't know anyone. And there were lots of trees.

Brian Kiley

Whenever I try to recall that long-ago first day at school only one memory shines through: my father held my hand.

Marcelene Cox

I didn't like school. They never gave me the present. They said they'd give me a present. They said: 'You're Laurie

We Don't Need No Education

Lee, ain't you? Well, you just sit there for the present.' I sat there all day but I never got it. I ain't going back there again!

Laurie Lee

When I graduated from first grade, all my dad did was tell me to get a job.

Frank, Billy Madison

My daughter told me she'd been learning the alphabet at school. 'What letter comes after T?' I asked. Without hesitation she replied, 'V.'

Ian Rose

I believe that schoolchildren should be given standardized national educational tests, and I will tell you exactly why: because I am not a schoolchild. I am strongly in favour of things that I, personally, do not have to do. Childbirth is another example.

Dave Barry

My father wanted me to have all the educational opportunities he never had so he sent me to a girls' school.

Eric Morecambe

Making Sense of School Prospectuses: Parental involvement encouraged: *Roped in for fund-raising activities*; Staff work as a team: *Headmaster usually having a nervous breakdown*; Extensive playing fields: *Property developers please note*; Modern teaching methods: *Classroom riots*.

John Koski and Mitchell Symons

I don't want to say anything against my kids, but I do go to PTA meetings under an assumed name.

Robert Orben

Fathers' Wit

– What's a library, Dad?
– Oh, it's just a place where homeless people go to shave and go to the bathroom.

Stevie and Peter Griffin, Family Guy

Children are smarter than any of us. Know how I know that? I don't know one child with a full-time job and children.

Bill Hicks

A schoolgirl was asked, 'In what countries are elephants found?' She answered, 'Elephants are very large and intelligent animals and are seldom lost.'

James Agate

A child supplies the power but the parents have to do the steering.

Dr Benjamin Spock

A happy childhood has spoiled many a promising life.

Robertson Davies

Every family should have at least three children. Then if one is a genius the other two can support him.

George Coote

A child prodigy is one with highly imaginative parents.

Will Rogers

I hate school shows. There's always some kid pounding a piano, and some four-eyed sissy torturing a violin and a fat slob reciting a poem about trees.

Archie Bunker, All in the Family

We Don't Need No Education

Prep schools are very democratic. You can't tell a millionaire's son from a billionaire's.

Vance Packard

– Dad, can I go to cookery school?
– Bobby, I know we've never talked about it, but someday I'm going to die. And on that day, you can go to cookery school.

Bobby and Hank Hill, King of the Hill

When your father tells you he wants you to amount to something, he means make a lot of money.

George Carlin

I talk and talk and talk, and I haven't taught people in 50 years what my father taught me by example in one week.

Mario Cuomo

I learned the way a monkey learns – by watching my parents.

Prince Charles

One father is more than 100 schoolmasters.

George Herbert

The greatest service a parent can render a child is to throw school reports unread into the waste-paper basket. Any success I have achieved has been due to my father's unflinching and inexplicable confidence.

Robert Morley

I continued to do arithmetic with my father, passing proudly through fractions to decimals. I eventually arrived at the point where so many cows ate so much grass, and tanks filled with water in so many hours. I found it quite enthralling.

Agatha Christie

Fathers' Wit

It's a myth that you will be able to help your kids with their homework. I'm taking remedial math so I can help my son make it to the third grade.

Sinbad

When I read my son's report card all I could say in his favour was that with those grades, he couldn't possibly be cheating.

Jacob Braude

My dad claimed he had a tough childhood. He told me he had to walk 20 miles to school in 5 feet of snow, and he was only 4 feet tall.

Dana Eagle

My dad told me he walked 10 miles to school in the snow, uphill both ways.

Anon

- When Abe Lincoln was your age, he walked 10 miles to school, split logs and studied by candlelight.
- When John Kennedy was your age, he was President.

Father and son

Parents should conduct their arguments in quiet, respectful tones, but in a foreign language. You'd be surprised what an inducement that is to the education of children.

Judith Martin

I will not allow my daughters to learn foreign languages because one tongue is sufficient for a woman.

John Milton

My kid drives me nuts. For three years now he's been going to a private school. He won't tell me where it is.

Rodney Dangerfield

We Don't Need No Education

– We have got to get Frederick into the Mulberry Academy. This may be the most important thing we ever do to ensure his happiness.
– Not counting our divorce.

Lilith Sternin and Frasier Crane, Frasier

Modern cynics and sceptics see no harm in paying those to whom they entrust the minds of their children a smaller wage than is paid to those to whom they entrust their plumbing.

John F. Kennedy

Racism isn't born, folks, it's taught. I have a 2-year-old son. You know what he hates? Naps. End of list.

Denis Leary

My father told me there's no difference between a black snake and a white snake. They both bite.

Thurgood Marshall

One woman said to my father, Nat 'King' Cole: 'You know, we don't want any *undesirables* in this neighbourhood.' And my father just looked at her and said, 'Well, if I see any I'll let you know.'

Natalie Cole

Groucho Marx was told that he would not be allowed to go into the swimming pool at a private club because it did not admit Jews. 'Well, my son is half-Jewish,' he replied, 'can he go in up to his waist?'

Gregory Smith

My father was very prejudiced; he never lived to see his dream of an all-Yiddish-speaking Canada.

David Steinberg

Fathers' Wit

My dad said, 'Son, it doesn't matter what race you are or the colour of your skin. There's always gonna be people out there who aren't gonna like you because you're irritating.'

Greg Rogell

Fathers send their sons to college either because they went to college, or because they didn't.

L. L. Hendren

As he waved me off to college, I'll never forget my dad's parting words. He said, 'Son, if there's anything you want, call me and I'll show you how to live without it.'

Will Collins

I believe that we parents must encourage our children to become educated, so they can get into a good college that we cannot afford.

Dave Barry

Driver Carries No Cash – He Has a Son in College.

Bumper sticker

'Sorry, Dad,' I said, 'I only got a third class degree. The lowest grade on the course. I've really let you down.' 'You haven't let me down, son,' my dad said. 'I never thought you'd pass.'

Johnny Vegas

If my own son, who is now 10 months, came to me and said, 'You promised to pay for my tuition at Harvard; how about giving me $50,000 instead to start a little business,' I might think that was a good idea.

William Bennett

– I'm going to college, son!
– Clown or barber?

Homer and Bart Simpson

The Birds and the Bees

SEX EDUCATION

These days when a father says, 'Son, I think it's time we had a little talk about sex,' the reply is apt to be, 'Okay, what did you want to know?'

Herbert Mumm

My father told me all about the birds and the bees, the liar – I went steady with a woodpecker till I was 21.

Bob Hope

Sex education was a dirty word when I was growing up. I didn't even know *National Geographic* ran pictures until I was married. Daddy always cut them out.

Erma Bombeck

Until I was 15 I was more familiar with Africa than my own body.

Joe Orton

Sex, like love, my father thought, had been greatly over-estimated by the poets. He would often pause at tea-time, his biscuit half-way to his mouth, to announce, 'I have never had many mistresses with thighs like white marble.'

John Mortimer

Fathers' Wit

The message about sex that she had got as a child was confused and contradictory. Sex was for men, and marriage, like lifeboats, was for women and children.

Carrie Fisher

There's a myth that humans should learn about sex from their parents. My relationship with my dad nearly ended when he tried to teach me to drive. I doubt our relationship would have survived if he'd had to instruct me how to operate my penis.

Bob Smith

Most of what I know about sex I learned from hanging around the gas station as a kid. The first couple of times I heard anyone ask, 'Getting any?' I thought they were talking about fish.

Lewis Grizzard

My parents were so resolutely chaste I assumed they must have bought me from a shop rather than indulging in the unsavoury business of conception.

Wendy Perriam

To conceive a child, my father told me, is as simple as blowing a feather off your knee.

John Cheever

I don't worry a lot about sex education in the schools. If the kids learn it like they do everything else, they won't know how.

Milton Berle

When Gary was 9, we had to see the school psychologist because he kept asking girls to do handstands for him.

Gary's dad, Men Behaving Badly

The Birds and the Bees

Now, girls, have I ever told you the facts of life? Stay away from boys 'cause they are all disgusting, self-indulgent beasts that pee on bushes and pick their noses.

Tom Wingo, The Prince of Tides

My 3-year-old came in and saw me getting out of the shower, naked. She said, 'Daddy, what's that?' She thinks it's a towel hook.

Bob Saget

My problems all boil down to how I learned about sex. When I was little I asked my father, 'What is a vagina?' He said, 'It's an aerial view of geese.' But then I asked, 'What's a clitoris?' He said, 'It's mouthwash.' So I've spent the rest of my life looking for three women who, by chance, happen to be walking in formation while gargling.

Richard Lewis

I don't believe in all this sex education. Let the kids today learn it where we did: in the gutter.

Pat Paulsen

My young son, Jack, asked me the dreaded question, 'Where do I come from, Daddy?' I decided not to fob him off, and gave him the full, frank explanation about sexual intercourse, orgasms and birth. 'Oh,' he said, 'I was just wondering, because the boy who sits in front of me comes from Jamaica.'

Paul LeBec

When my 4-year-old daughter asked where babies come from, I thought she was too young for a frank explanation, so I gave her the whole bit about 'Daddy planted a seed in Mummy's tummy.' Then one day just as

Fathers' Wit

I was trying to reverse the car into a tight parking space with a queue of traffic behind me she asked, 'Daddy, did you plant the seed with your hand or did you use a trowel?'

Nick Cavender

As I congratulated a friend on his marriage, my young son turned to him and said, 'When are you going to give your pollen to her?'

Christian Lorimer

— What are Uncle Jesse and Aunt Becky doing in the bedroom?
— They're, uh, they're doing their taxes.
— Are they going to do their taxes every night?
— Only for the first couple of months of their marriage.

Michelle Tanner and Joey Gladstone, Full House

— … and then Mommy kissed Daddy, and the angel told the stork, and the stork flew down from heaven, and put the diamond in the cabbage patch, and the diamond turned into a baby!
— Our parents are having a baby too. They had sex.

Little girl and Wednesday Addams, Addams Family Values

My father once attempted to give a very straightforward account of the whole reproductive process. To his amusement, I rushed out of the room to be sick before he was half finished.

John Osborne

I'm Irish Catholic, so my father never discussed women and sex with me. We talked about sandwich meat.

Conan O'Brien

The Birds and the Bees

I didn't know the facts of life until I was 17. My father never talked about his work.

Martin Freud, son of Sigmund

Telling a teenager the facts of life is like giving a fish a bath.

Arnold Glasgow

Children today know more about sex than my father or I ever did.

Jon Reed

– I found our son's bag full of porno tapes.
– I guess that shows he's interested in sex. Or film-making.

Helen and Gil Buckman, Parenthood

We must make our boys understand the difference between making a baby and being a father.

William Raspberry

We all tell our kids how babies are made but it's just as important to tell them how babies are prevented.

Wesley Crane

Things children should know – but don't: that Mummy and Daddy don't actually do all that *just* to make a baby.

Katharine Whitehorn

The best sex education for kids is when Daddy pats Mommy on the bottom when he comes home from work.

Dr William H. Masters

Children used to ask their parents where they came from; now they tell them where to go.

Harry Day

Fathers' Wit

– Jack's up in his room planning his future.
– The only thing he's planning is his next wank – whether he's going to use his left hand or his right.

Ozzy and Sharon Osbourne

Please knock before entering your teenage son's room, as the disruption of a youth who is spanking his monkey will be twice as traumatic for you as it is for him.

Esquire *magazine*

– Stop that, son, you'll go blind!
– I'm over here, Dad!

Anon

It's a fallacy that males stop masturbating after 17. Most usually stop after one.

Jeff Green

Fatherhood trumps gayness. As gay parents of son, Erez, we tried our best: we played him Judy Garland records and showed him tapes of *West Side Story* but his inclinations remain resolutely heterosexual.

Jesse Green

Never come out to your father in a moving vehicle.

Kate Clinton

Father warned me about men, but he never said anything about women.

Tallulah Bankhead

Dating

I've got a bit of a situation at home. My eldest daughter brought a boy home for the first time. And I think it's safe to say I reacted rather badly. She said, 'Hello, Dad, this is Billy.' I said, 'Billy? Billy is it?' and I went up to this person and said, 'If you so much as fucking touch her I'll cut you.' This Billy started crying. Still, that's 7-year-olds for you.

Phill Jupitus

I never paid much attention to those parenting books. I just skipped to the chapters on how to keep your kids from having sex.

Paul Hennessy, 8 Simple Rules for Dating My Teenage Daughter

– How do you feel about your daughters dating? Are you good about that?
– Well, we have a deal where they're not allowed to have sex until after I'm dead. So, so far, it's been fine.

Interviewer and Billy Crystal

– What the hell is that you've got on?
– A dress.
– Says who?
– Calvin Klein.

Mel and Cher Horowitz, Clueless

– Hold it. You're not going out like that. I can see your bra and that slingshot you're wearing.
– It's a thong.
– It's floss.

Paul and Bridget Hennessy, 8 Simple Rules for Dating
My Teenage Daughter

Fathers' Wit

Red nail polish? Why don't we just buy you some rouge, high heels and a lamppost?

Archie Bunker, All in the Family

Watching your daughter being collected by her date feels like handing over a million-dollar Stradivarius to a gorilla.

Jim Bishop

So, you're my daughter's date. Let me warn you – anything happens to my daughter, I've got a .45 and a shovel. I doubt anybody would miss you.

Mel Horowitz, Clueless

You better be delivering a package because you sure as hell aren't picking anything up.

Paul Hennessy, 8 Simple Rules for Dating My Teenage Daughter

When one of my daughter's boyfriends comes over to the house I just say, 'See that little girl over there? She's my life. So if you have any thoughts about hugging or kissing, you remember these words: I've got no problem going back to prison.'

Bill Engvall

My daughter's boyfriends? I figure if I kill the first one, word will get out.

Charles Barkley

When your daughter's date shows up, casually show him your collection of five shrunken heads, then yell up to your daughter, 'Honey, Number Six is here!'

David Letterman

I would hear the slam of a car door, the turn of a key in the lock, but never saw my daughter's boyfriends. One day it

finally dawned on me – she wasn't hiding them from me –
she was hiding me from them.

Iain Parker

In high school, my sister went out with the captain of the
chess team. My mom and dad loved him. They figured that
any guy that took two hours to make a move was okay
with them.

Brian Kiley

Drive carefully, kids. And don't forget to fasten your
condoms – *seatbelts*, I mean seatbelts.

George Banks, Father of the Bride

My dad told me, 'Never sleep with a girl if you're going to
be embarrassed to be seen on the street with her the next
day.' I think that was more for the girl's benefit than mine.
He didn't want me jumping on some girl and then leaving
her in the lurch.

Ronald Reagan Jr

My dad was a cop, so dating was a total nightmare. The
police escort I could handle, but the loudhailer from the
helicopter was a bit much … 'Keep both hands on the
steering wheel where we can see them.'

Sandi Selvi

Dad, *promise me* you won't say to this one, 'I used to change
her nappies, you know.'

Lara Ryan

– I assure you I said nothing wrong to your date. All I said
  was, 'Hi there, I'm Janey's dad.' That was all.
– Dad, your flies were open the whole time!

Ben and Janey Harper, My Family

Fathers' Wit

I introduced a girlfriend to my parents once and my dad said, 'Pleased to meet you – how much do you earn?'

Sanjeev Bhaskar

Prince William is wonderful. When I met him at the Queen's Jubilee Concert I said, 'I have got a daughter for you.'

Ozzy Osbourne

What do women want? I always heard that women secretly want their fathers. So I used to walk around in a 1950s business suit, with a pipe and hat. My opening line was, 'You should be getting to bed.'

Conan O'Brien

My father always said, 'Be the kind they marry, not the kind they date.' So on our first date, I'd nag the guy for a new dishwasher.

Kris McGaha

My dad told me, 'Marry a girl who has the same beliefs as the family.' I said, 'Dad, why would I want to marry a girl who thinks I'm a schmuck?'

Adam Sandler

I'm looking for a guy just like my dad, who orders dentures through the mail and takes great pride in the fact that his eyebrows meet.

Judy Tenuta

Never date a woman whose father calls her 'Princess'. Chances are she believes it.

Anon

Bad luck is meeting your date's father and realizing he's the pharmacist you bought condoms from that afternoon.

Lewis Grizzard

Dating

My father used to say, 'Be home by midnight, or, by God, sleep on the porch!'

Oprah Winfrey

Darlene is late. I'm gonna go out and stand in the middle of the street so the first thing she sees when she pulls up is my head exploding.

Dan Conner, Roseanne

– Do you know how late it is?
– Daddy, a watch doesn't really go with this outfit.

Mel and Cher Horowitz, Clueless

My fiancée's father said to me, 'If you're going to be my son-in-law, you need not go on calling me Sir. Call me Field Marshal.'

John Betjeman

You'll have many, many friends, but if your relationship with your mate is 100 per cent of your heart, you'll never need a friend.

Bill Cosby

At your first dinner party with your son and new daughter-in-law, it's not a good idea to tell her the way your mother used to prepare the dish.

David Letterman

One of life's greatest mysteries is how the boy who wasn't good enough to marry your daughter can be the father of the smartest grandchild in the world.

Anon

Following in Father's Footsteps

WORK

Some of us will want to follow in father's footsteps … but we can't sign on for ever can we?

Pauline Campbell-Jones, The League of Gentlemen

Growing up, my father told me I could be whoever I wanted. What a cruel hoax! I'm still his son.

Ken Smith

My father was an eminent button maker – but I had a soul above buttons – I panted for a liberal profession.

George Colman

At the unemployment exchange, my father gave his occupation as an astronaut but not prepared to travel.

Roy Brown

– My father was a nun. I know, because whenever he was up in court, and the judge used to say, 'Occupation?', he'd say, 'Nun.'

Baldrick, Blackadder Goes Forth

For the first time in my life – I was then 11 years old – I felt myself forced into an open opposition. No matter how hard and determined my father might be about putting his own plans and opinions into action, his son was no less obstinate in refusing to accept ideas on which he set little or no value. I would not become a civil servant.

Adolf Hitler

Following in Father's Footsteps

Being a member of parliament is the sort of job all working-class parents want for their children – clean, indoors, and no heavy lifting.

Diane Abbott, MP

– Our son says he wants to be a magician.
– He might be good at it. He certainly made 20 years of our lives disappear.

Susan and Ben Harper, My Family

When I was growing up, my father told me I'd make a great waiter. They never come when you call them.

Bob Monkhouse

My dad told me I should work for an airline: I'm always late and I lose things.

Nick Stein

I remember when I took you for your first tetanus shot, son. You were about five or six. When the nurse gave you the shot, you took your mind off it by listing the names of all of Puccini's operas. Right then I knew you'd never be a cop like me.

Martin Crane, Frasier

Lisa, if you don't like your job you don't go on strike. You just go in every day and do it really half-assed. That's the American way.

Homer Simpson

My son has taken up meditation. At least it's better than sitting doing nothing.

Max Kaufman

Fathers' Wit

Whatever happened to the good old days when children worked in factories?

Emo Philips

My daughter, aged 7, asked me what I did at work. I told her I worked at a college and my job was to teach people how to draw. She stared at me, incredulous, and said, 'You mean they forgot?'

Howard Ikemoto

My dad doesn't draw Bugs Bunny. He draws pictures of Bugs Bunny.

5-year-old son of Chuck Jones, animator

My father invented the burglar alarm, but it was stolen from him.

Victor Borge

Dad, you've taken a job as a Santa in the mall? You must really love us to sink so low.

Bart Simpson

My father wanted me to become a doctor, but I wanted to do something more creative, so we compromised and I became a hypochondriac.

Wally Wang

After my father was cast as the Cowardly Lion in *The Wizard of Oz* he was typecast as lion.

Bert Lahr

My father played the viola in the Royal Danish Symphony Orchestra. A lot of people don't know the difference between a violin and a viola. Unfortunately, my father was one of them.

Victor Borge

Following in Father's Footsteps

William Pitt the Younger is not only a chip off the old block but the old block itself.

Edmund Burke

I'm a doctor and picking up my 5-year-old daughter, Chloe, from nursery one day, I left my bag and stethoscope on the back seat of my car. She started playing with the stethoscope and I began wondering, could my daughter be destined to follow in my footsteps? Then she spoke into the instrument, 'Welcome to McDonald's. May I take your order?'

Mark Miller

She got her looks from her father. He's a plastic surgeon.

Groucho Marx

My father invented a cure for which there was no disease, and unfortunately, my mother caught it and died of it.

Victor Borge

Often Daddy sat up very late working on a case of Scotch.

Robert Benchley

I work as my father drank.

George Bernard Shaw

My dad was the town drunk. Usually that's not so bad, but New York City?

Henny Youngman

My dad always said, 'The day I can't do my job drunk is the day I turn in my badge and gun.'

Lewis Kiniski, The Drew Carey Show

Fathers' Wit

Every small boy wonders why his father didn't go into the ice cream business.

Anon

I was an only child. Raised in the country. Each autumn, my father would gather in the harvest. I never really understood why because he was an accountant by profession.

Harry Hill

I just received the following wire from my generous daddy: 'Dear Jack, Don't buy a single vote more than is necessary. I'll be damned if I'm going to pay for a landslide.'

John F. Kennedy

I tell my sons, 'I don't care what you do in life, but whatever you do, be the best person in the world when you do it. Even if you're going to be a ditch digger, be the best ditch digger in the world.'

Joseph P. Kennedy

The day after the elections, my nanny said, 'Your father's upstairs. You can call him "Mr President" now.'

Caroline Kennedy

My brother, Bob, doesn't want to be in government – he promised Dad he'd go straight.

John F. Kennedy

As long as I've been in the White House, I can't help waking at five in the morning and hearing the old man at the foot of the stairs calling and telling me to get out and milk the cows.

Harry S. Truman

Following in Father's Footsteps

Manual labour to my father was not only good and decent for its own sake but, as he was given to saying, it straightened out one's thoughts.

Mary Ellen Chase

I watched a small man with thick calluses on both hands work 15 and 16 hours a day. He taught me all I needed to know by the simple eloquence of his example.

Mario Cuomo

Statistics show that attendance at work is better among married men with children and spikes even higher among fathers of newborns. Quite a coincidence, huh?

Thomas Hill

If I was an employer, I'd employ nothing but fathers – they always want an excuse to work late.

Julie Burchill

– My dad's a headhunter.
– Cool! Does he cut them off with a chainsaw?

Harry Gough and Tim Right, The Right Stuff

My father was a soldier who, after 30 years of service, was catapulted to the rank of corporal.

Woody Allen, Take the Money and Run

My father 'went to the office'. What he did when he got to the office was a blank. He might have walked off the edge of the world each morning, returning at six with the *Evening Standard*.

Robert Robinson

My dad was the fastest man in the world. He didn't finish work until five o'clock and he was always home by two.

Ken Dodd

Fathers' Wit

I used to eat quite a lot of fast food. When my daughter, Chelsea, started preschool and she was asked what her father did, she said that he worked at McDonald's.

Bill Clinton

Most kids at school had accountants for dads. Mine was the archetypal rock 'n' roller, in the band Status Quo. I kept away from music for a long time but now my dad's my biggest fan. He said, 'I'm pleased you're not crap.'

Rick Parfitt Jr

My father always told me, 'Find a job you love and you'll never have to work a day in your life.'

Jina Fox

My father said to me, 'Never do a job that can be replaced by machines.' So I thought being an actor was a job that can't be replaced by machines. But it looks as though we might be getting nearer to that stage.

Michael Caine

My mother said, 'You children must be extra polite to strangers because your father's an actor.'

Dorothy Fields

My father, Dario Argento, directs horror movies in Italy and sometimes I think he gave me life because he needed a lead actress for his films.

Asia Argento

I'll never forget my father's response, when I told him I wanted to be a lawyer. He said, 'If you do this, no man will ever want you.'

Cassandra Dunn

Following in Father's Footsteps

My father wanted me to be a lawyer but I told him I was going into the theatre, which is the same job, really – but less dangerous to my fellow men.

Peter Ustinov

Daddy's a litigator. Those are the scariest kind of lawyers. Daddy's so good he gets $500 an hour to fight with people. But he fights with me for free because I'm his daughter.

Cher Horowitz, Clueless

A triumph of my father's salesmanship was the time he sold a Mexican both an ice pack and a hot water bottle, neither of which he came in for.

Richard Armour

Every time I'm about ready to go to bed with a guy, I have to look at my dad's name all over the guy's underwear.

Marci Klein, daughter of Calvin Klein

The mill's closed, children. There's no more work. We're destitute. I'm afraid I have no choice but to sell you all for scientific experiments.

Father, Monty Python's The Meaning of Life

– Has fatherhood affected your song writing in any way?
– Well, it's harder to find the ashtrays.

Tom Waits

There is no more sombre enemy of art than the pram in the hall.

Cyril Connolly

Nobody ever asks a father how he manages to combine marriage and a career.

Sam Ewing

I became president of Fox Movies when I was 22 years old because my father gave me the studio as a birthday present.

Richard Zanuck

The average man will bristle if you say his father was dishonest, but he will brag a little if he discovers that his great-grandfather was a pirate.

Bern Williams

My father taught me to work; he did not teach me to love it. I never did like to work, and I don't deny it. I'd rather read, tell stories, crack jokes, talk, laugh – anything but work.

Abraham Lincoln

No man on his deathbed ever looked up into the eyes of his family and said, 'I wish I'd spent more time at the office.'

Anon

Our Father Who Art in Heaven

RELIGION

Our Father, who aren't in Heaven,
Harold be thy name …

Emily, aged 4

I am determined that my children shall be brought up in their father's religion, if they can find out what it is.

Charles Lamb

At bottom, God is nothing more than an exalted father.

Sigmund Freud

Our Father Who Art in Heaven

And people tell me Jesus wasn't Jewish. Of course he was Jewish! Thirty years old, still living at home with his parents, working in his father's business, his mother thought he was God's gift ...

Robin Williams

My parents raised me in the Jewish tradition. I was taught never to marry a Gentile woman, shave on Saturday and, most especially, never to shave a Gentile woman on Saturday.

Woody Allen

My father is Catholic, my mother Jewish. When I went to confession, I'd pray, 'Bless me, Father, for I have sinned ... and I think you know my lawyer, Mr Cohen.'

Bill Maher

I do want to have Brooklyn christened, but I'm not sure which religion.

David Beckham

– We have to have Brady baptized. He has to wear a dress.
– Baby's first drag show!

Miranda Hobbes and Carrie Bradshaw, Sex and the City

I'd be the worst possible godfather. I'd probably drop her on her head at the christening. I'd forget all her birthdays until she was 18. Then I'd take her out, get her drunk and, quite possibly, try to shag her.

Will, About a Boy

It is almost nicer being a godfather than a father, like having white mice but making your nanny feed them for you.

T. H. White

Always a godfather – never a god!

Alexander Woollcott

Fathers' Wit

Now listen to me. We're going to go to church as a family and we're going to have a damn nice Sunday, d'you hear me?

Red Foreman, That 70s Show

Father's religious requirements – that the service come from Cranmer's rites in the old prayer book, that it take 33 minutes or less, that the church be within 10 minutes' driving distance and that the altar be sufficiently simple that it wouldn't remind him of a gift shop – limited his choice of parishes.

Susan Cheever

When Father went to church and sat in his pew, he felt he was doing enough. Any further spiritual work ought to be done by the clergy.

Clarence Day

Attending his first church service, my son turned to me and said, 'Daddy, when's the interval?

Edward Price

My father considered a walk among the mountains as the equivalent of churchgoing.

Aldous Huxley

The one thing Father always gave up for Lent was going to church.

Clarence Day

To impress upon us what the loss of the soul through mortal sin meant, my father would light a match, grab our hands and hold them briefly over the flame, saying, 'See how that feels? Now imagine that for all eternity.'

Pat Buchanan

Men made God in their own image, and he's a deadbeat dad. Never sends money, doesn't come to visit, can't get him on the phone.

Mimi Gonzalez

Empty Nest

This is the hardest truth for a father to learn: that his children are continuously growing up and moving away from him (until, of course, they move back in).

Bill Cosby

I call my son the boomerang kid because he keeps on moving back.

Ross Cooper

There isn't a child who hasn't gone out into the brave new world who eventually doesn't return to the old homestead carrying a bundle of dirty clothes.

Art Buchwald

– Michael's almost 16. We're about to stop parenting.
– Parenting never stops.
– Don't you *ever* say that!

Ben Harper and headmaster, My Family

Parenting is like your Aunt Edna's ass. It goes on for ever and it's just as frightening.

Frank Buckman, Parenthood

A Jewish man with parents still alive is a 15-year-old boy, and will remain a 15-year-old boy until they die.

Philip Roth

Fathers' Wit

Some people seem compelled by unkind fate to parental servitude for life. There is no form of penal service worse than this.

Samuel Butler

My kids seem to regard me as a life-long Father Christmas.

Harry Burton

– Aren't you worried about empty nest syndrome? All of a sudden you'll be standing there with your wife, and the house will be empty, and there'll be no sounds?
– And we'll have sex! Real *loud*. And nobody knocking on our door!

Interviewer and Bill Cosby

When I went to college, my parents threw a going-away party for me – according to the letter.

Emo Philips

Though we have raised you for this moment of departure and we're very proud of you, a part of us longs to hold you once more as we did when you could barely walk – to read you just one more time *Goodnight Moon*.

Bill Clinton, at daughter Chelsea's high school graduation ceremony

Every one of your letters I read first for the facts and the fun – and then a second time to see how the red inside heart of you is ticking.

Carl Sandburg

Let your children go if you want to keep them.

Malcolm Forbes

My mam always says, 'Drive carefully … give me three rings when you get in.'

Peter Kay

Empty Nest

Thomas Wolfe wrote, 'You can't go home again.' You can, but you'll get treated like an 8-year-old.

Daryl Hogue

No one can feel like CEO of his or her life in the presence of the people who toilet-trained her and spanked her when she was naughty. We may have become Masters of the Universe yet we may still dirty our diapers at the sound of Daddy's growl.

Frank Pittman

I get along great with my parents. I still talk to them at least once a week. It's the least I can do. I still live in their house.

David Corrado

Human beings are the only creatures on earth that allow their children to come back home.

Bill Cosby

My kids are grown, and lately I find myself starting to think I'd rather see No Children sections in restaurants than No Smoking ones.

Bill Geist

It's only when you grow up and step back from your father, or leave him for your own career and your own home – it's only then that you can measure his greatness and fully appreciate it. Pride reinforces love.

Margaret Truman

Fathers' Wit

Papa Don't Preach

FATHERLY ADVICE

Son, three little sentences will get you through life:
Number 1: Cover for me. Number 2: Oh, good idea, Boss!
Number 3: It was like that when I got here.

Homer Simpson

Be very good. Do not bump yourself. Do not eat
matches. Do not play with scissors or cats. Do not forget
your dad. Sleep when your mother wishes it. Love us
both. Try to know how we both love you. That you will
never learn.

Richard Harding-Davis, in a letter to his 9-month-old daughter

My father always said, 'Never write anything down that you
wouldn't want published on the front page of the *New York
Times*.'

Ted Kennedy

With my father there was no such thing as half-trying.
Whether it was running a race or catching a football,
competing in school – we were to try our best. 'After
you have done the best you can,' he used to say, 'the hell
with it.'

Robert F. Kennedy

Kennedys don't cry.

John F. Kennedy

Dad told all the boys to get laid as often as possible.

John F. Kennedy

Papa Don't Preach

'Never trust a man who doesn't drink,' was one of my father's favourite expressions, and he died plenty trustworthy.

Les Patterson

Never put anything on paper, my boy, and never trust a man with a small black moustache.

P. G. Wodehouse

Daddy said, 'Always make friends with people who are smarter than you are. And in your case it won't be difficult.'

Jim Drake

As you journey through life, son, you will encounter all sorts of nasty little upsets, and you will either learn to adjust yourself to them or gradually go nuts.

Groucho Marx

My son keeps complaining about headaches. I keep telling him, 'When you get out of bed, it's feet first.'

Henny Youngman

It was on my fifth birthday, my dad put his hand on my shoulder and said, 'Remember, son, if you ever need a helping hand, you'll find one on the end of your arm.'

Sam Levinson

Father told me if I ever met a lady in a dress like yours, I must look her straight in the eye.

Prince Charles

Now, son, you don't want to drink beer. That's for daddies and kids with fake IDs.

Homer Simpson

Fathers' Wit

My father used to say, 'Never accept a drink from a urologist.'

Erma Bombeck

Dad taught me how to climb up a tree. But not how to climb down.

Mark Finch

My dad always used to tell me that if they challenge you to an after-school fight, tell them you won't wait – you can kick their butt right now.

Cameron Diaz

My dad told me, 'Don't go looking for trouble, but if you find it, make damn sure you win.'

John Wayne

You've got to face the bullies, son, take a risk, hit back. Should I speak to the boy from my immense superior strength and size? What's that, speak to his father? His father's a boxer? Well now, let's not be hasty. We don't want to descend to his level, do we?

Alan Brien

The important thing I learned from my father was to find your own bone and sink your teeth in it.

William Plummer

Son, you tried to do something and you failed. What's the lesson here? Never try.

Homer Simpson

The most important thing parents can teach their children is how to get along without them.

Frank Clark

Papa Don't Preach

I owe a lot to my parents, especially my mother and father.

Greg Norman

When my kids are preparing for a night out, I give them a little fatherly advice: 'Don't get drunk or stoned tonight. I'll be fucking pissed off because I can't! And if you're gonna have sex, wear a condom.'

Ozzy Osbourne

My dad used to say, 'Always fight fire with fire,' which is probably why he was thrown out of the fire brigade.

Harry Hill

Dad always said that honesty was the best policy and money isn't everything. He was wrong about other things too.

Sam Buckley

Dad taught me everything I know. Unfortunately, he didn't teach me everything he knows.

Al Unser

When my father caught me imitating him by pretending to smoke a toy pipe he advised me very earnestly never to follow his example in any way; and his sincerity so impressed me that to this day I have never smoked, never shaved, and never used alcoholic stimulants.

George Bernard Shaw

My father said, 'Smoking won't hurt you as long as you do it in moderation. And that goes for everything else you do, too.' I've been smoking since I was 17, and except for the fact that I usually feel awful, I'm fit as a fiddle.

Arthur Marx, son of Groucho

Fathers' Wit

If my father told us not to do something, he didn't do it either. A lot of people tell their kids not to smoke cigarettes and they smoke cigarettes.

Madonna

I phoned my dad to tell him I had stopped smoking. He called me a quitter.

Jo Brand

It was a maxim with our revered father – 'Always suspect everybody.'

Charles Dickens, The Old Curiosity Shop

When I was a small boy, my father told me never to recommend a church or a woman to anyone. And I have found it wise never to recommend a restaurant either. Something always goes wrong with the cheese soufflé.

Edmund Love

The best advice I was ever given was on my 21st birthday when my father said, 'Son, here's a million dollars. Don't lose it.'

Larry Niven

I have found out that the best way to give advice to your children is to find out what they want and then advise them to do it.

Harry S. Truman

My father taught me to regard him as a warning and not a model ... and I now see that this anxiety on his part was admirable and lovable; and that he was really just what he so carefully strove not to be: that is, a model father.

George Bernard Shaw

Papa Don't Preach

My father used to say, 'Superior people never make long visits.'

Marianne Moore

Dad told me, 'Work your way up or rust your way out.'

Gerald Harbin

My dad taught me the difference between a flathead and a Phillips screwdriver, and when you forge your father's name on a letter for school to make certain he will never find out.

Luke Wood

'If you don't go to other men's funerals,' Father said, 'they won't go to yours.'

Clarence Day

My dad said, 'You'll never be someone because you procrastinate.' I said, 'Just you wait.'

Ted Carnes

My dad said I'd never amount to anything. Lucky guess.

David Cousins

My dad used to say, 'Keep your chin up, son.' He once broke his jaw walking into a lamppost.

Adam Sandler

My father always used to say that when you die, if you've got five real friends, then you've had a great life.

Lee Iacocca

My father said, 'If, at the end of your life, you can count all your friends – your really good friends – on just one hand, then you've been spending a lot of time alone in your room.'

Bob Saget

Fathers' Wit

Dad always said, 'Babe, pay your own way. Don't owe anybody anything.' And that's the way I've lived.

Lily Tomlin

My son, do not talk to your company of melancholy things such as sores, infirmities, prisons, trials, war, and death. Do not recount your dreams. Do not attempt to correct the faults of others, especially as that is the duty of fathers, mothers and lords.

Hugh Blair

My father told me I should make a point of trying every experience once – except incest and folk dancing.

Leo Fallon

The best advice ever given me was from my father. When I was a little girl, he told me, 'Don't spend anything unless you have to.'

Dinah Shore

The best advice my father gave me was, 'If you stop punching her, she'll let go of your hair.'

Terry Firth

My old father used to have a saying: If you make a bad bargain, hug it all the tighter.

Abraham Lincoln

Every father should remember that one day his son will follow his example instead of his advice.

Anon

My dad used to say, 'It's not a sin to be skint, but it's a sin to look skint.'

Alan Ball

Papa Don't Preach

My son, take care to have your stocking well gartered up, and your shoes well-buckled; for nothing gives a more slovenly air to a man than ill-dressed legs.

Lord Chesterfield

My father used to say, 'Let them see you and not the suit. That should be secondary.'

Cary Grant

Advice to son: Never confuse 'I love you' with 'I want to marry you.'

Cleveland Amory

Dad used to say, 'No matter how smart a girl is, she can't be that smart if she's dating you.'

Artie, Norm

My father gave me some good advice before I got married. 'Son,' he said, 'never do anything once around the house that you don't want to do the rest of your life.'

Anon

Around the time I made *9½ Weeks,* I was doing lots of interviews in which I talked frankly about sex. My dad sent me a can of tennis balls with this note taped to it: 'Dear Kim, when you give an interview and the feeling of being outrageous is present, place one of these balls in your mouth. If you are still able to say "oral sex" after doing this, then you are hopeless. Love from your loving father better known as Daddy.'

Kim Basinger

My father used to say that we must surrender our youth to purchase wisdom. What he never told me was how badly we get cheated on the exchange rate.

Morris West

Fathers' Wit

Son, a man's never wrong doing what he thinks is right.

Ben Cartwright, Bonanza

My dad used to tell me, 'You're never as good as they say you are when they say you're good, and you're never as bad as they say you are when they say you're bad.' And once you understand that, you can survive.

George Clooney

My father, Denis, was fond of saying, 'Better to keep your mouth closed and be thought a fool than to open it and remove all doubt.'

Carol Thatcher

My dad taught me, 'What you see is what you get – except in pre-packaged strawberries.'

H. Jackson Brown Jr

My father taught me the importance of quality workmanship. 'Measure twice, cut once,' was one of his many mottoes.

Chris Hilliard

Twenty years from now you will be more disappointed by the things you didn't do than by the ones you did do. So throw off the bowlines. Sail away from the safe harbour. Catch the trade winds in your sails. Explore. Dream. Discover.

Mark Twain

I was able to overcome shyness with some great advice from my father. He told me, 'Son, always walk into a room as though you belong there and people will believe you do.'

Ed McMahon

My dad always said, 'If you don't stand for something, you'll fall for anything.'

Jimmy Osmond

Don't take life or its happenings too seriously. Lift up the corners of that mouth that I gave you one moonlit night. Never let yourself *hate* any person. It is the most devastating weapon of one's enemies. Always remember that your dad is liable to call you all sorts of names when he disapproves of your behaviour, but don't take him too seriously, and always come to him – whatever your difficulty – he may be able to help you. Impossibly, he may not be as stupid as he looks. Forget all the above and remember only that I would love to kiss you twenty-one times and give you a million dollars.
     Your hopeless Dad

Father of Katharine Hepburn, advice in a letter to her
on her 21st birthday

My father taught me that the most powerful weapon you have is your mind.

Andrew Young

Son, never seem more learned than the people you are with. Wear your learning like a pocket watch and keep it hidden. Do not pull it out to count the hours, but give the time when you are asked.

Lord Chesterfield

Don't carry a grudge. While you're carrying a grudge, the other guy's out dancing.

Buddy Hackett

My dad, Tony Richardson, used to repeat a line of Samuel Beckett's so often that I had it pinned on my wall at home: 'Keep on failing. Only this time fail better.'

Joely Richardson

Fathers' Wit

My father died when I was 15. The advice I remember the most, he'd always say, 'Be a man,' which meant 'Take it. Take it like a man.'

Billy Crystal

Always be a little kinder than necessary.

J. M. Barrie

Think the best of people, do not dwell upon their faults and try not to see them. You will be happier for it.

Mark Twain

I learned from the example of my father that the manner in which one endures what must be endured is more important than the thing that must be endured.

Dean Acheson

Whenever I was in trouble, Dad would say, 'Step over the body and keep moving.'

Ralph Grigson

The only fatherly advice I have ever given is not to eat your peas off a knife.

John Cheever

My father once said, 'Nearly half the troubles you have in life are caused by what goes in and what comes out of your mouth.'

Arthur Reubens

I was always terrified of what my father was going to say to the press. When they asked him what he thought of the permissive society he said he wished to God it had been invented 60 years ago.

Edward Heath

Papa Don't Preach

Knowledge of the world is only to be acquired in the world, and not in a closet.

Lord Chesterfield

Don't get aggravated when your old dad calls you his baby, because he always will think of you as just that – no matter how old or big you may get.

Harry S. Truman

Dad always thought laughter was the best medicine, which I guess is why several of us died of tuberculosis.

Jack Handey

I've always followed my father's advice. He told me, first, to keep my word, and, second, to never insult anybody unintentionally. So if I insult you, you can be goddamn sure I intend to.

John Wayne

From my mother I learned to make piecrusts and to iron shirts. From my father I learned to catnap and to tell the time without a watch.

Verlyn Klinkenborg

Son, you get out of it what you put into it.

Earl Woods

My father didn't tell me how to live; he lived, and let me watch him do it.

Clarence B. Kelland

I remember my young brother once saying, 'I'd like to marry Elizabeth Taylor,' and my father said, 'Don't worry, your turn will come.'

Spike Milligan

Fathers' Wit

How true Daddy's words were when he said, 'All children must look after their own upbringing.'

Anne Frank

My father gave me the greatest gift anyone could give another person: he believed in me.

Jim Valvano

When things get really tough there are the final, most potent words of wisdom a father can have, 'Go ask your mother.'

Frank Lancaster

Daddy's Little Girl

FATHERS AND DAUGHTERS

You have a girl. Unless I cut the wrong cord.

Dr Kosevich, Nine Months

When we had a little girl, all of a sudden I couldn't remember that I ever wanted to have a boy.

Henry Louis Gates

I am glad it is a girl: all little boys ought to be shot.

Reverend Sydney Smith

What are little girls made of?
What are little girls made of?
Sugar and spice
And all things nice,
That's what girls are made of.

Nursery rhyme

Daddy's Little Girl

If our child is a boy, he is to be named James; if a girl, it would be kinder to drown her.

Evelyn Waugh

It is only rarely that one can see in a little boy the promise of a man, but one can almost always see in a little girl the threat of a woman.

Alexandre Dumas

The fortunate man has a daughter as his first-born.

Spanish proverb

Daughters, I think, are always easier for fathers. I don't know why.

William Plummer

I only have two rules for my newly born daughter: she will dress well; she will never have sex.

John Malkovich

Friends ask if there's a difference between having a son or a daughter. No doubt about it, the day my daughter was born everyone began to look like a potential molester to me … 'She's not sitting on *your* lap.'

Jack Coen

Things a father should know: how to flirt with a small daughter (very important) without making his wife feel like a discarded bedrock.

Katharine Whitehorn

Three daughters and people ask, 'Were you upset that the third daughter was a girl?' I say, 'No, not at all. I'm whittling a boy out of wood right now.'

Bob Saget

Fathers' Wit

Little girls are the nicest things that happen to people.

Alan Beck

I dedicate this book to my daughter Leonora without whose never-failing sympathy and encouragement it would have been finished in half the time.

P. G. Wodehouse

A young lady is a female child who has just done something dreadful.

Mike Taylor

When it comes to little girls, God the father has nothing on father, the god. It's an awesome responsibility.

Frank Pittman

I was raised by my dad. When I was 13 and got my period, I had to tell him I needed tampons. 'Harpoons? What the hell does a girl your age need with harpoons,' he said.

Rosie O'Donnell

Dad raised me to get outside, get muddy, and most of all – get on with it.

Sarah Ferguson, Duchess of York

I'm grateful to my father for making me a tough son-of-a-bitch. It helps me deal with situations.

Lana Zanocchio, daughter of Mafia godfather Anthony Graziano

Past experience indicates that the best way of dealing with my daughter is total attention and love.

Lyndon B. Johnson

It isn't that I'm a weak father, it's just that Jane's a strong daughter!

Henry Fonda

Daddy's Little Girl

I live with a French woman and my four daughters. I live with all these females and not one of them can cook. I'm so sick of the female sensibility. I know they have to be on the phone all the time but do they have to have all these lipsticks and bottles everywhere? And the smells! Why can't women smell of something that isn't a smell?

Bob Geldof

The father of a daughter is nothing but a high-class hostage. A father turns a stony face to his sons, berates them, shakes his antlers, paws the ground, snorts, runs them off into the underbrush, but when his daughter puts her arm over his shoulder and says, 'Daddy, I need to ask you something,' he is a pat of butter in a hot frying pan.

Garrison Keillor

I know I have my father, Charlton, wrapped around my little finger but he has us wrapped around his.

Holly Heston

Daddy, never Dad. Mummy became Mum at some point, but Daddy has always been Daddy.

Louise Hunt

My dear Anne, it would be in vain for me to try to send you any news. I can only send you my love, and that is anything but news. It is as old as you are.

Henry Wadsworth Longfellow

Nobody in this world can make me so happy, or so miserable, as a daughter.

Thomas Jefferson

Fathers' Wit

Daughters! They're a mess no matter how you look at 'em. A headache till they get married – if they get married – and after that they get worse … Either they leave their husbands and come back with four kids and move in your guest room or the husband loses his job and the whole caboodle come back. Or else they're so homely that you can't get rid of them at all and they sit around like Spanish moss and shame you into an early grave.

William Demarest, The Miracle of Morgan's Creek

There is a special bathroom in heaven for the father of girls.

Tommy Birch

I didn't have the balls to vote against my father, Ronald Reagan, but I couldn't vote for him.

Patti Davis

Things not to worry about: don't worry about popular opinion; don't worry about dolls; don't worry about the past.

F. Scott Fitzgerald, letter to his daughter

I have three daughters and I find as a result I played King Lear almost without rehearsal.

Peter Ustinov

It is admirable for a man to take his son fishing, but there's a special place in heaven for the father who takes his daughter shopping.

John Sinor

Tiger Lily calls me Dad. We were out shopping the other day and they played one of my songs then one by her dad,

Michael Hutchence. She said, 'My real dad's a better singer than you, Dad.' I just said, 'Sheesh … Thanks.'

Bob Geldof

A father is always making his baby into a little woman. And when she is a woman he turns her back again.

Enid Bagnold

A doting father is not simply surprised when his little girl grows up, he is crushed.

Victoria Secunda

Love is wonderful. Until it happens to your only daughter.

Tagline, Father of the Bride

Psychiatrists say girls tend to marry men like their fathers. That is probably the reason mothers cry at weddings.

Bernadette Ellis

My older daughter has been living away from home for well over a decade now. She has a steady boyfriend and we get on just fine. But every so often, when I see them together, a strange urge comes over me to sit him down and ask him if his intentions are honourable.

Jon Carroll

You worry about your daughter meeting the wrong kind of guy, the guy who only wants one thing, and you know exactly what that one thing is, because it's the same thing you wanted when you were their age. Then you stop worrying about her meeting the wrong guy, and you worry about her meeting the right guy. That's the greatest fear of all because then you lose her.

George Banks, Father of the Bride

Fathers' Wit

The father of the bride is a pitiable creature. Always in the way – a sort of backward child – humoured but not participating in the big decisions. His only comfort is a bottle of bourbon.

Dean Acheson

I was so proud of you and thrilled at having you so close to me on our long walk in Westminster Abbey, but when I handed your hand to the Archbishop I felt that I had lost something very precious.

George VI to Princess Elizabeth, on her wedding

He who has daughters is always a shepherd.

Spanish proverb

Your son is your son till he takes a wife, but your daughter is your daughter for all of your life.

Spencer Tracy, Father of the Bride

Like Father, Like Son

FATHERS AND SONS

– It's like a dream come true. A son. Somebody to carry on the proud name of Rubble. D'ya think I'll make a good dad, Fred?
– Well, sooner or later you have to find *something* you're good at.

Barney Rubble and Fred Flintstone, The Flintstones

Like Father, Like Son

It is funny the two things most men are proudest of is the thing that any man can do and doing does in the same way, that is being drunk and being the father of their son.

Gertrude Stein

A man's desire for a son is usually nothing but the wish to duplicate himself in order that such a remarkable pattern may not be lost to the world.

Helen Rowland

If ye want a boy, dae it wi' your boots on.

Scottish saying

What are little boys made of?
What are little boys made of?
Frogs and snails,
And puppy-dogs' tails,
That's what boys are made of.

Nursery rhyme

Which are harder to raise, boys or girls? Has to be girls. Boys are easy. Give them a box of matches and they're happy.

Milton Berle

The fact that boys are allowed to exist at all is evidence of a remarkable Christian forbearance among men.

Ambrose Bierce

I have always thought that the initial trouble between me and my father was that he couldn't see the slightest purpose in my existence.

Laurence Olivier

Fathers' Wit

There are to us no ties at all in being a father. A son is distinctly an acquired taste.

Heywood Broun

Perhaps host and guest is really the happiest relationship for father and son.

Evelyn Waugh

It is not flesh and blood but the heart which makes us fathers and sons.

Johann Schiller

I am often asked whether it is because of some genetic trait that I stand with my hands behind, like my father. The answer is that we both have the same tailor. He makes our sleeves so tight that we can't get our hands in front.

Prince Charles

A boy is Truth with dirt on its face, Beauty with a cut on its finger, Wisdom with bubble gum in its hair and Hope of the future with a frog in its pocket.

Alan Beck

When you can't do anything else to a boy, you can make him wash his face.

Ed Howe

- Whoa, whoa, settle down, son.
- Mom was just telling a story I don't want to hear any more.
- Well, that's no reason for you to go running out of the room screaming like a maniac.
- It was about her having her period.
- As you were.

Dan and D. J. Conner, Roseanne

Like Father, Like Son

You know as soon as you have a son, he's going to hit you in the balls at least once or twice a year, if you're lucky. They claim it's an accident. I don't think so. There are piñatas that get hit less than my balls.

Dennis Miller

Fathers and sons show more consideration towards one another than mothers and daughters do.

Friedrich Nietzsche

Bobby, if you weren't my son, I'd hug you.

Hank Hill, King of the Hill

There's nothing wrong with a father kissing his son … I think.

Homer Simpson

– Dad, I thought it was good to be a man.
– Oh, no, son. Not since the 1960s.

D. J. and Dan Conner, Roseanne

One night, a father overheard his son pray: 'Dear God, make me the kind of man my daddy is.' Later that night, the father prayed, 'Dear God, make me the kind of man my son wants me to be.'

Anon

– Where on earth did we get our son?
– I don't know. I was sleeping.

Ben and Susan Harper, My Family

The worst waste of breath, next to playing the saxophone, is advising a son.

Kin Hubbard

Fathers' Wit

I didn't hire Scott as assistant coach because he's my son. I hired him because I'm married to his mother.

Frank Layden

It was our son who kept our marriage together: neither of us wanted custody of him.

Chubby Brown

What strikes me as odd is how much my father managed to get across to me without those heart-to-hearts which I've read about fathers and sons having in the study or in the rowing-boat or in the car. Somehow I understood completely how he wanted me to behave, in small matters as well as large.

Calvin Trillin

> Blessings on thee, little man
> Barefoot boy, with cheek of tan!
> From my heart I give thee joy –
> I was once a barefoot boy!

John Greenleaf Whittier

Boyhood is the natural state of rascality.

Herman Melville

My son, Ben, was almost always in the same nondescript suit as though he never realized that other clothes were actually on the market.

Harold Nicholson

I never got along with my dad. Kids would come up to me and say, 'My dad can beat up your dad.' And I'd say, 'Okay. When?'

Bill Hicks

Like Father, Like Son

- Your dad's great.
- Yeah, in a parallel universe where my hair is straight and so are you.

Will and Grace, Will and Grace

I had dinner with my father last night, and made a classic Freudian slip. I meant to say, 'Please pass the salt,' but it came out, 'You prick, you ruined my childhood.'

Jonathan Katz

My therapist and I have really bonded. Even he hates my father now.

Terence Davies

A boy may hate his father, but he always respects him.

Louis B. Mayer

Lizzie Borden took an axe
And gave her mother forty whacks;
When she saw what she had done
She gave her father forty-one!

American rhyme

Marriage? I take a cold-hearted look at my parents' life and the urge passes.

Drew Carey

Son, you're even dumber than I tell people.

Frank Barone, Everybody Loves Raymond

Son, let this be a lesson to you: never do tequila shooters within a country mile of a marriage chapel.

Al Bundy, Married … With Children

Fathers' Wit

My eldest son is about to become 21, and all I can say is that he makes me feel incredibly old. He is an incredible help and assistance to me as I become increasingly decrepit.

Prince Charles on Prince William

– An only son, sir, might expect more indulgence.
– An only father, sir, might expect more obedience.

Oliver Goldsmith

Never fret for an only son. The idea of failure will never occur to him.

George Bernard Shaw

Father thought a day out huntin' taught you much more than a day at school.

Dick Francis

It was always important to me to lead my children into real woods, not the woods of Little Red Riding Hood.

Norman Maclean, A River Runs Though It

My father knew the constellations. He showed me Venus, the evening star, Aries the ram, how to find the North Star if I was ever lost in the woods. I never got lost in the woods, but I loved those times and never even knew it.

James Dodson

– Isn't this great? Just you and me, together, hunting. Son, I want you to forget that I'm your father for a minute. I want you to tell me exactly what you think of me.
– How about I do this when you're not holding a gun?

Red and Eric Foreman, That 70s Show

Like Father, Like Son

– Hi, Dad, I was just planning the father-son river-rafting trip.
– Heehee. You don't have a son.

Bart and Homer Simpson

In my family, there was no clear division between religion and fly-fishing.

Norman Maclean, A River Runs Through It

My father took me fishing once. He marched me to the riverbank and snapped a picture of me with a fishing rod in my hand, then we went home.

Andrei Codrescu

– Come along, son, we're gonna go on a fishing trip.
– Why? What did I do wrong?

Len and Tom Hogan, Sierra

Fishing is boring, unless you catch an actual fish, and then it's disgusting.

Dave Barry

It took me 17 years to finally get round to taking my son fishing, as every father should do once in his life. Every time we'd tried to go before, everyone was throwing up on the boat so we had to turn back.

Ozzy Osbourne

When I was around 7, we went fishing and couldn't catch anything, so Dad took out his machine gun and said, 'You know what? We'll shoot 'em.' He let me pull the trigger. 'Well, we still didn't get any,' Dad said afterward, 'but we scared the hell out of 'em.'

Jack Floyd, son of 'Pretty Boy' Floyd

A man knows he is growing old because he begins to look like his father.

Gabriel García Márquez

I turned on the TV in a hotel room and there was a movie I was in. I watched for a while and thought, hey, I'm not a bad actor. Only later did I realize it was my son, Michael.

Kirk Douglas

I don't mind looking into the mirror and seeing my father.

Michael Douglas

You can't compare me to my father. Our similarities are different.

Dale Berra, son of Yogi

I cheat my boys every chance I get. I want to make 'em sharp. I trade with the boys and skin 'em and I just beat 'em every time I can.

William A. Rockefeller

There must always be a struggle between a father and son, while one aims at power and the other at independence.

Samuel Johnson

Anything further, Father? That can't be right. Isn't it, Anything father, further?

Groucho Marx

Life Lessons for Fathers

After my wife left me, I thought about killing myself. I wrote two lists, one with reasons to stay alive, the other with reasons to end it. The Why Bother? list was two pages. The Why Stay? list was two words: the children.

Bob Geldof

No man can possibly know what life means, what the world means, what anything means, until he has a child and loves it.

Lafcadio Hearn

While we try to teach our children all about life, our children teach us what life is all about.

Anon

Shall I tell you something strange? Well, when I became a father I understood God.

Honoré de Balzac

Fatherhood has made me less selfish. Once you become a father you stop being the picture and become the frame.

Daniel Lang

At the birth of your child, you forgive your parents *everything*, without a second thought, like a velvet revolution. This is part of the cunning of babies.

Martin Amis

Before Josh and Rebecca, I merely strode through the world like a man. Now I crawl, hunker, scramble, hop on one foot, often see the world from my hands and knees.

Hugh O'Neill

Seeing my kids growing up brings back some of the joys of childhood – sticky fingers, running until you're out of breath, laughing so hard that your stomach hurts.

Neil Layton

Fathers' Wit

You have a boy or a girl of your own and now and then you remember, and you know how they feel, and it's almost the same thing as if you were your own self again, as young as you could remember.

James Agee

You have to ask children and birds how cherries and strawberries taste.

Johann Wolfgang von Goethe

Living with Katie is like living with a 24-hour-a-day Zen master.

Samuel Shem

The value of marriage is not that adults produce children but that children produce adults.

Peter de Vries

You must allow room for disagreement. I always encouraged Tiger to question what I was saying and, if he found me in error, to let me know so I could learn, too. In this way, parents can learn from their children.

Earl Woods

You can learn many things from children. How much patience you have, for instance.

Franklin P. Jones

By the time a man realizes that maybe his father was right, he usually has a son who thinks he's wrong.

Charles Wadsworth

Older Fathers

Up until now, it's been a safe bet that John Humphrys has never appeared in the same sentence as Clint Eastwood and Jack Nicholson. Yes, the correct answer is they have all fathered children in their 50s and 60s.

Phil Hogan

Rediscovering fatherhood a second time, I am finding that like youth, it is wasted on the young.

Arthur Miller

I had my first son when I was 18. I was young and stupid and I grew up with the children. Having a son at 60, when I'm older and established, means that I can wallow in the parenthood thing.

Paul Hogan

Congratulations are in order for Woody Allen – he and Soon Yi have a brand new baby daughter. It's all part of Woody's plan to grow his own wives.

David Letterman

Catherine Zeta is the mother; I'm the official burper.

Michael Douglas

If you have a 2-year-old around the house, it keeps you thinking, keeps you young, watching the learning process.

Clint Eastwood

Some rules about late fatherhood: don't be tempted to grow a 'youthful' pony-tail (the rule is: if it hangs, someone will swing on it); don't ask the children from your first marriage to baby-sit – they'll only compare birthday presents; do try to take it on the chin when the other mums and dads at school mistake you for grandpa.

Phil Hogan

– What a man you are, maestro. You had children in your seventies!
– Yes, but I couldn't pick them up!

Interviewer and Pablo Picasso

The great thing about being a 78-year-old father is that when Baby cries all night, you can't hear a thing. And no need for expensive toys once Baby discovers the fun tufts of hair growing out of your ears. Also, you get a great feeling of togetherness sharing a dish of strained peas.

David Letterman

There are advantages to becoming parents when you're older: going to the movies will be economical – one child and two seniors.

George Banks, Father of the Bride, Part II

Absent Fathers

– Jane. It's been a long time.
– Yes.
– How are the children?
– We didn't have any children.
– Yes, of course.

Lieutenant Frank Drebin and Jane Spencer, The Naked Gun 2½:
The Smell of Fear

Absent Fathers

My mother and father didn't get divorced though I begged them to.

Allan Felix, Play it Again, Sam

My ex-husband is suing me for custody of the kids, so now I have to go to court and fight him because my lawyer says it would look really bad if I don't.

Roseanne Barr

When I was 10 my pa told me never to speak to strangers. We haven't spoken since.

Steven Wright

When mom got mad she'd threaten, 'Wait 'til your father gets home.' 'Mom,' I'd say, 'it's been eight years.'

Brett Butler

I spent the first 20 years of my life waiting for two men I was reasonably certain would never come back – my daddy and Jesus Christ.

Brett Butler

After Simon Raven had broken with his wife she telegraphed: 'WIFE AND BABY STARVING.' Simon is supposed to have wired back: 'EAT BABY.'

Frances Partridge

My father came and went like the tide.

Olivia Harris

My father died when I was 8. At least that's what he told us in the letter.

Drew Carey

Fathers' Wit

My father died in childbirth.

Woody Allen

The one thing my absent father taught me, that he doesn't even know he taught me, was that I didn't want to be like him.

Bernie Mac

- D'you think the reason I'm screwed up about men is because my dad walked out on us?
- My father came home at seven on the button every night and I still have no clue.

Carrie Bradshaw and Miranda Hobbes, Sex and the City

Like most fathers at that time, my father wasn't there, but, in a way, that can be a blessing. Familiarity breeds contempt.

Jack Ford

A man who does not spend time with his family can never be a real man.

Mario Puzo

I wanted to spend more time with my family, but I found my family didn't want to spend more time with me.

Greg Dyke

David Blunkett has resigned as Home Secretary to spend time with someone else's family.

Ronnie Corbett, Have I Got News for You

Remembering Dad

It doesn't matter who my father was; it matters who I remember he was.

Anne Sexton

I remember watching TV with my dad; wrestling and jumping up and down with him in my room. We did a lot of drawing. He would scribble circles and squiggles on a piece of paper, and I would have to turn it into whatever I saw in them. With him, every day was an adventure. It was like my dad and I were buddies, and there was no real sorrow then.

Sean Lennon on John Lennon

To this day I cannot see a bright daffodil, a proud gladiolus, or a smooth eggplant without thinking of Papa. Like his plants and trees, I grew up as a part of his garden.

Leo Buscaglia

When I think of my father, Ronald Reagan, the memories that bubble to the surface are not of policy or politics. They are of the man who opened a child's imagination, who taught her to be a good horsewoman and to always get back on when I fell off.

Patti Davis

I can remember playing under the big wooden desk in my father's office. My mother didn't like us to chew gum, so we'd go into his office and he'd feed us gum under the desk.

John F. Kennedy Jr

Fathers' Wit

I went through Old Spice, Hai Karate, but what I really remember is the smelly stuff my father used to wear. English Leather. The fatherly cologne, yeah, with that wooden top. Sneaking some of his English Leather, spraying it on myself, I'll never forget that.

Michael Jordan

I can't remember my father at all. I can remember my mother only through a child's eyes. I don't know which fact is the sadder.

Clive James

I'd been told of all the things you're meant to feel when your father dies. Sudden freedom, growing up, the end of dependence, the step into the sunlight when no one is taller than you and you're in no one's shadow. I know what I felt. Lonely.

John Mortimer

The mature, 45-year-old woman, quite experienced in matters of life and death, knows that it was 'for the best', but Daddy's girl, who hung on to his belt and danced foxtrots on the tops of his shoes, cannot accept that Daddy is not here any more.

Mary-Lou Weisman

Even now, 21 years after my father died, not a week goes by that I don't find myself thinking I should call him.

Herb Gardner

My dad died in 1990 and I've had the same dream every night since. I die and go down a tunnel of light, to a room filled with light. My dad walks in and says, 'Joe! Did you leave all these lights on?'

Joe Ditzel

My mother goes to a séance every Friday night since my father died just so she can still yell at him.

Chuck Lumley, Night Shift

My mother and I once paid out for a séance in Widnes. We wanted to contact my father because we were going camping and couldn't lay hands on the mallet.

Victoria Wood (as Kitty)

This is a moment that I deeply wish my parents could have lived to share. My father would have enjoyed what you have so generously said of me; and my mother would have believed it.

Lyndon B. Johnson, speech at Baylor University

When I think of my dad, I get this Obi-Wan Kenobi voice in my head, but instead of giving me words of wisdom and advice, it just says things like, 'Ouch, my back!' and 'Pull my finger. Just pull it.'

Lori Chapman

I never put aside the past resentment of the boy until, with my own sons, I shared his final hours, and came to see what he'd become, or always was – the father who will never cease to be alive in me.

Jimmy Carter

My Heart Belongs to Daddy

LOVE

I'm going to tell you something that I didn't learn until I became a father. You don't just love your children. You fall in love with them.

Frasier Crane, Frasier

When a healthy 3-year-old child says, 'I love you' there is meaning in it like that between men and women who love and are in love.

D. W. Winnicott

One can love a child, perhaps more deeply than one can love another adult, but it is rash to assume that the child feels any love in return.

George Orwell

Fatherly love is the ability to expect the best from your children despite the facts.

Jasmine Birtles

Parental love is the only real charity going. It never comes back. A one-way street.

Abbie Hoffman

A child hasn't a grown-up person's appetite for affection. A little of it goes a long way with them.

George Bernard Shaw

A child's spirit is like a child, you can never catch it by running after it; you must stand still, and, for love, it will soon itself come back.

Arthur Miller

My Heart Belongs to Daddy

It wasn't until my daughter was 2 years old and realized she was stuck with me that she said, during a walk through autumn leaves, 'I love you.'

James Thurber

Sorry, honey, I can't take you to the mall. Daddy loves you, but Daddy also loves *Star Trek*, and in all fairness, *Star Trek* was here first.

Peter Griffin, Family Guy

Kids spell love, T-I-M-E.

John Crudele

The overwhelming reason why *The Osbournes* is successful is the fact – and I picked this up from people that stop me in the street because I don't watch the show myself – it's obvious that we love each other.

Ozzy Osbourne

Men love their children, not because they are promising plants, but because they are theirs.

Charles Montagu

If I were in America I could say, 'I love you, Dad,' the way they do in the films. But in Limerick, they'd laugh at you. In Limerick, you're only allowed to say you love God, and babies, and horses that win. Anything else is softness in the head.

Frank McCourt, Angela's Ashes

My father's not the warm and fuzzy kind. He can't bring himself to ask about feelings and emotions. All he ever asks is, 'How's the car?'

Dana Eagle

Fathers' Wit

Children need love, especially when they don't deserve it.

Harold Hulbert

You don't really understand human nature unless you know why a child on a merry-go-round will wave at his parents every time around – and why his parents will always wave back.

William D. Tammeus

We find delight in the beauty and happiness of children that makes the heart too big for the body.

Ralph Waldo Emerson

My father was so important to me. He reached in and put a string of lights around my heart.

Patricia Charbonneau, Desert Hearts

I loved my father. I looked for his faithful response in the eyes of many men. None could say 'for ever' as he did.

Patricia Neal

'I love you more than God,' my father once told me. This was serious; he was a religious man. I don't know if he meant he loved me more than he loved God or more than God loved me. It almost doesn't matter. Whichever he meant, he was right.

Mary Gordon

We love our kids, but there are times when we don't really like them, or at least we can't stand what our children are doing. But most of us keep those feelings to ourselves, as if it's a dirty little secret. It doesn't fit in with our images of what we should do or feel.

Lawrence Kutner

My Heart Belongs to Daddy

Unlike the male codfish, which suddenly finding itself the parent of 3,500,000 little codfish, cheerfully resolves to love them all, the British aristocracy is apt to look with a somewhat jaundiced eye on its younger sons.

P. G. Wodehouse

After I stopped riding, I put on a lot of weight. When I lost it again, I asked my father, 'Do you love me more now I've lost weight?' He said, 'Yes.' It was so much the wrong answer.

Clare Balding

I love my dad, Steve Tyler, although I'm definitely critical of him sometimes, like when his pants are too tight. We have slumber parties, and when we can't sleep we stay up all night trading beauty tips. He knows all about the good creams and masks.

Liv Tyler

I loved my father but I hated him, too. He was a ragman who drove a horse and wagon and couldn't read or write. But to me he was big. He was strong. He was a man. I didn't know what I was. But I wanted to be accepted by him.

Kirk Douglas

We never know the love our parents have for us till we have become parents.

Henry Ward Beecher

—Y'know, Dad, I never say anything nice to you. I'm always going on at you for picking your nose and farting … You and m'mam … more than anything.

Denise Royle, The Royle Family

Fathers' Wit

It's a wonderful feeling when your father becomes not a god but a man to you – when he comes down from the mountain and you see he's this man with weaknesses. And you love him as a human being, not as a figurehead.

Robin Williams

I love you all, kids! I love you more than life itself. But you're all fucking mad!

Ozzy Osbourne